Ludwig van Beethoven

Play by Play

Ludwig van Beethoven

Play by Play

by
Alan Rich

with performances by
Chicago Symphony
Orchestra
Sir Georg Solti, conductor

A Newport Classic CD/B™
Presentation

HarperCollinsSanFrancisco,
1995

Credits

Executive Producer for the Series: *Lawrence J. Kraman*

Series Editor: *Jackson Braider*

Analytical Indexing: *John Ostendorf, Rudolph Palmer, Christopher Woltmann*

Art Direction: *Ann E. Kook*

Interior Design: *Stuart L. Silberman*

This recording was originally released on the London label, # 430 087-2.

Library of Congress Cataloging-in-Publication Data

Rich, Alan.
    Ludwig van Beethoven : play by play / by Alan Rich ; with
    performances by Chicago Symphony Orchestra, Sir Georg Solti, conductor.
    p. cm.
    "A Newport Classic CD/B presentation."
    Discography:
    Includes bibliographical references (p.156).
    ISBN 0-06-263545-X
    ISBN 0-06-263552-2
    1. Beethoven, Ludwig van, 1770-1827. 2. Beethoven, Ludwig van, 1770-1827.
    Symphonies, no. 3, Op. 55 E-Major. 3. Beethoven, Ludwig van, 1770-1827.
    Egmont. Overture. 4. Music Appreciation.

ML410.B4R44 1995   94-49111
780' .92—dc20   CIP
                                                      MN

95 96 97 98 99 ❖ RRD(C) 10 9 8 7 6 5 4 3 2 1

Contents

A Note from the Executive Producer

IT IS NOT WITHOUT SOME IRONY that we have chosen to call the *Play by Play* series a "CD/B" presentation. Where the race is on in computer circles to define the *next* multimedia delivery system—though the various parties involved have never actually agreed as to what the current one is—we have concocted this marriage between two very different media, invented at least one millenium and half-a-world apart. It is, as you can see, very much a *low-tech* affair: a book and a compact disc.

Mind you, we have always been very conscious of the fact that this is a new medium. It isn't just a book with a CD pasted into it for fun, nor it is a CD with a hefty set of liner notes. Each illuminates the other; each brings something to the other what it might otherwise lack, particularly as regards the exploration, the appreciation, the *understanding* of music.

I feel a bit like Cecil B. DeMille in all of this: yes, the CD/B has been ten years in the making, but the cast has certainly not been in the thousands. Clayton Carlson and Bill Crowley, of HarperCollins and PolyGram respectively, caught on very quickly, and without their enthusiastic support, it is fair to say that none of this would have happened. The people in both their organizations—James McAndrew, Leslie Clagett, Justine Davis—have all been absolutely wonderful to work with.

Somewhere along the way, classical music became *serious* music, and when that happened, many of us lost touch with the idea that this music—heavy and heady as it can be sometimes—was very often supposed to be delightful, a pleasure, a source of enlightenment. I hope that this series will open up for you what has been, up to this point, a very closed world.

LAWRENCE J. KRAMAN

Author's Note

AS AN UNDERGRADUATE at Harvard, slogging my way through a pre-med major but with my heart in the Music Department, I learned to think about the listening experience as an ongoing narrative, full of thrills and surprises. The wonderful G. Wallace Woodworth would start a Haydn symphony on the 78-rpm record player, then pick up the tone arm and make us guess what was going to happen next. (We were usually wrong, but that wasn't the point.) I learned about the momentum of Beethoven's *Ninth Symphony* from Donald Tovey's measure-by-measure "précis" in the first volume of his Essays in Musical Analysis (omitted, for reasons not fathomable, in the current reprint edition of these essential musical insights). Woody in the classroom, and Tovey on paper, have shaped the way I think about listening to music over half a century. Now, however, I don't have to dash to the piano to play Tovey's musical squibs; I can hand them off, second-by-second or CD index-by-index, as clearly as if Woody were still up front running the Victrola. You can, too; that's what Play by Play will do for you, for me, and for music.

ALAN RICH
LOS ANGELES, 1995

How to Use
This Book

THE CD included in this volume has been analytically indexed. That is to say, within each track on the compact disc there has been embedded a series of inaudible codes that allows the listener to access particular moments in the composition, be it something as quick as the entry of the bass part in a fugue or something as fundamental as the start of the recapitulation section in a sonata.

The various CD player manufacturers all have developed their own particular way of accessing the index points on a compact disc and the reader should consult his or her manual for the appropriate instructions. Some older models of machines have no such capacity. However, the trick in using the sections of this book devoted to Analytical Indexing—the Play by Play section and the Essential Recordings section immediately following it—is to look at the tracking display on the CD player and relate it to what you are reading about in the book.

Here is a typical example of what will appear in the text: [T2/i3, 1:29]. This provides the reader three pieces of information: the track (T2), the index point (i3), and the absolute time of the event in the track (1:29). What this shorthand describes, then, is the third index point on the second track of the compact disc, which occurs at 1:29 into the track. So, even if your CD player doesn't have indexing, the time display will give you a precise indication of the moment a particular event being described in the text will occur.

Enter Beethoven: The Musical World in 1770

JOHANN SEBASTIAN BACH had been dead for twenty years, virtually forgotten except by a few scholars and connoisseurs of antiquity. George Frideric Handel had been dead for eleven years, but his memory remained bright and honored—if not in his native Germany, at least in his adopted England. Like everything else in the world in the latter half of the eighteenth century, music was in a state of flux, one that was agonizing and exhilarating.

The fires of revolution swept the landscape. England's American colonies were stirring uneasily under the royal yoke; the infant Beethoven was only a few months old, in his native Bonn, when a gang of Bostonian activists half a world away dumped chests of His Majesty's tea into their harbor to protest taxation. But the revolutionary spirit expressed itself in ways other than the force of arms; it seemed a time when practically every artistic and social value that mankind had once held dear and inviolable was now up for reexamination. The final tomes of Denis Diderot's twenty-eight-volume *Encyclopédie* were under way in 1770; Samuel Johnson's Dictionary attempted the same redefining process for English readers; Jean Jacques Rousseau had already denounced the arts as the great corrupting force of the age; Johann Joachim Winckelmann's essays on classical art influenced designers and architects from Thomas Jefferson's Monticello to Vienna's Karlskirche. Change was in the air. Beethoven, music's supreme innovator, chose the right time to be born.

Music itself underwent an enormous set of changes. The very notion of consumership, of public events where one bought a ticket and went into a concert hall and took a seat, only came about midway into the eighteenth century. Johann Christian Bach, the youngest of Johann Sebastian's sons and far more famous during his own lifetime than his father had been in his, virtually invented the public concert, with a London series he began in 1765 which offered some fifteen concerts a year of chamber and orchestral music, most of it brand-new. Before the time of these events, and of similar projects in Berlin, Hamburg, and Paris, concert music had been a far more private affair, presented in the palaces and gardens of the aristocracy for the delight of invited guests. One heard choral music in the churches, of course, and vocal music at the opera, but the idea of the public concert, given over to the connoisseurship of music for music's sake, was as revolutionary a concept as democracy itself.

The idea caught on. Europe's major cities became yet another revolutionary battleground, thanks to the infighting among rival producers of series of chamber and orchestral concerts. With the new concert audience came a new range of tastes. After the complexity of all that uplifting music at weekly church services, or the high emotion as one operatic diva battled another for a place in the opera-house spotlight, the new audience succumbed in its secular pursuits to a kinder, gentler music meant for easy listening. They demanded it in the concert room, and they took it home as well. The musical amateur (in the best sense, from the Latin *amare*, "to love") came into his (or her) own. The new musical taste was, if anything, a two-faceted monster. On the one hand, the crowd flocked passionately to the latest fashionable virtuoso—especially if he happened to be a dimpled *Wunderkind* like, say, the six-year-old Wolfi Mozart. On the other hand, they hunted down a whole repertory of easy-to-play music for the family parlor, for the bourgeois equivalent of the nobleman's musicales, with a few friends invited over—after the dinner dishes had been cleared—for a little *Hausmusik*.

What was behind this newly minted passion for domesticated music and public virtuosi? Partly it was the emergence of a new social force—in Europe, and shortly thereafter, in America as well: the educated middle class. Spurred on by the libertarian writings of Voltaire and Rousseau, the populace by 1770 seemed seized with an obsession for self-improvement and knowledge. Add to this the writings of the archeologist and art historian Winckelmann, whose immensely popular essays on the purity of ancient architecture redefined the essence of classicism in terms the new bourgeoisie could understand and relate to, and one begins to detect the light behind this whole age of enlightenment.

If those were the social forces that defined the new cultural consumership, there were practical considerations as well. The success of the pianoforte in eighteenth-century Europe was an explosive force that might be compared to the passion for the compact disc today. It wasn't so

The "Pastoral" Symphony inspired a quantity of romanticized portraits of the composer, atypically taking his ease. Here, a photo-engraving by Hafstaengl after a painting by L. Schmid.

much that the instrument superseded the former harpsichord and clavichord in terms of tone and dynamics; it did eventually, after a few false starts. More important, it could be mass-produced, and therefore affordably priced, as harpsichords never could. By the 1780s, an Austrian family could install in its proudest room a fairly reputable locally made piano for anywhere from 175 to 600 florins—the equivalent of $40 to $140. Measure that against Mozart's statement, that he could support himself and his wife Constanze in modest bourgeois circumstances for 1200 florins a year, and it works out that a piano in 1780 cost about the same percentage of a year's salary as it does today!

Inevitably, the piano in the home demanded a steady diet of new music. If the newfangled instruments could be mass-produced cheaply, the same held true for printed sheet music. In 1755, the Leipzig firm of Breitkopf & Härtel had perfected a way of printing music from movable type, enabling cheap mass publication. The floodgates were thereby opened, and the European household was awash in music.

If the daughter of the family was the one most often granted the privilege of music lessons, virtually every composer worth his salt hastened to provide the young lady with music "easy and pleasant, for the beginner as well as the expert." The solid bourgeois composer Johann Wilhelm Hässler went so far as to audition his new sonatas before an assemblage of young ladies, begging them to "notify me of any unpleasantnesses, so that they may be altered for the benefit of my *interessées.*"

No time in musical history produced anything like the bulk of new works that inundated the European market in the closing decades of the eighteenth century. The elegant clarity of typical classical style, with its unwritten but widely honored rules of musical structure, made composition easy, in a sense. Yet two geniuses rise above the craftsmanlike ordinariness of the minor Classical masters; they, too, knew all the rules but also knew when and how to break them for the sake of expression and originality. One worked in comfort for most of his life and reaped the honors due the greatness of his music. The other worked in relative discomfort, enmeshed for most of his life in the political deception that sometimes, even today, turns geniuses suicidal.

In 1770, Franz Joseph Haydn, thirty-eight, was already in the fourth year of his enlightened employment as composer to the Esterházy family in eastern Austria. He had composed five masses, sixteen string quartets, and forty symphonies, with the further pleasure of having at his disposal a private orchestra that was rumored to be one of the best in Europe. His music had begun to circulate

Beethoven and the Piano

Beethoven made his first impact on Viennese society not as a composer, but as a pianist. Contemporary accounts endow his playing with words like "volcanic" and "tumultuous," a far cry from the elegance of Mozart and his generation, but certainly appealing in their directness. Above all, Beethoven astounded audiences with his improvisations, picking up on a tune suggested by the audience on the spot, and carrying it through permutations, uphill and down, for as long as it pleased him. Constanze Mozart asked him to play the solo part in her late husband's *D-minor Piano Concerto (No. 20)* at a memorial concert on 31 March 1795, and the cadenzas he improvised for that performance were later written down; they offer a fair example of the breadth and originality of his powers of departure from a given work into the stratosphere. So does the long, rambling piano exordium that begins that most curious of all of Beethoven's concoctions, the *Fantasy, Op. 80,* for piano, orchestra, vocal soloists, and chorus.

No piano was safe when Beethoven was around. Friends who had been enlisted to turn pages for him ended up, instead, repairing bro-

beyond the Austro-Hungarian borders, and his quartets were performed in some of Vienna's most aristocratic homes.

Wolfgang Mozart was fourteen that year; he, too, could point to a fair body of work already, including two operas, several masses, and nearly twenty symphonies. His father Leopold, a renowned violinist and composer, had dragged his prodigy son from one European capital to another for several years, and the boy earned the acclaim due a child prodigy, one or two steps up from the praise customarily lavished on a particularly adept chimpanzee. Now, at fourteen, he

---

ken strings and hammers. The small pianos of the time cramped his imagination; this can be seen in some of the sonatas, where a theme that was to be repeated in a higher key had to be altered because the keyboard didn't encompass those notes. (*The E-major Sonata, Op. 14, No. 1,* is a case in point.)

He constantly pestered piano manufacturers (who in Vienna, at the time, were as numerous as tabby cats) to upgrade their instruments to his standards, but got nowhere. By the time a piano worthy of his musical visions arrived—in 1818, a huge, gorgeous one from the London firm of Broadwood—he

was too deaf to hear it. Even so, he created the sweeping *Hammerklavier Sonata* to celebrate his new acquisition. He sat at the instrument for hours, furiously banging away. The instrument maker Johann Andres Stumpff called on Beethoven and was proudly escorted to the Broadwood. "Quite a sight confronted me," he reported in some horror. "The upper registers were mute, the broken strings in a tangle, like a thorn bush whipped by a storm."

Yet Beethoven continued to make music at his piano, so profound that only he could hear it.

Beethoven's birthplace was a comfortable middle-class residence.

stood on the threshold of life as a mature composer. He was to glean a certain amount of fame, but it was earned against odds that Haydn never experienced.

They came together, after Mozart had moved on from his native Salzburg and determined to buck the treadmill in Vienna, and Haydn recognized the genius in his younger colleague far sooner than did the rest of the world. "Before God and as an honest man," he once remarked to Leopold Mozart, "your son is the greatest composer known to me…"

Haydn's streak of benevolence and generosity is not every musician's way of acting toward others in the profession—not in Haydn's time, nor today. It becomes a part of the Beethoven story as well. Retired from the Esterházy post and traveling to further fame and acclaim in a concert series in London, Haydn had been advised to stop off in the German provincial city of Bonn, to check out a promising young musician named Beethoven, who might be worthy of his patronage.

That is where this story begins.

The Bonn Years

THE RIVER RHINE has always been the fountainhead of legend. Its own beauty, carving a path past the green Taunus highlands, past rich vineyards and pasture land as it sweeps from the Alps to the sea, richly colored those legends. "In these valleys, mythology grafts itself to the legends of the saints," wrote Victor Hugo, "and strange results are produced, fantastical flowers of the imagination… sounds of harps in the thickets, melodious songs chanted by invisible singers, hideous laughter emitted by mysterious wayfarers."

Late in the eighteenth century, the city of Bonn, located on the Rhine about twenty-four kilometers south of Cologne, was known chiefly as the seat of the Electorate and Archbishopric of Cologne. Johann van Beethoven, whose Flemish father had resettled his family in Bonn, earned his living as a singer in the electoral chapel; his wife, Maria Magdalena Laym, was the daughter of the head cook at

The birth of Beethoven: A fanciful interpretation of the event, with the Muses and a chorus in attendance, ready to perform the Ninth Symphony.

the nearby palace of Ehrenbreitstein. They had married in 1767. Their first child died in infancy; Ludwig was the second, his birth registered on 16 December 1770. Of several later children, only two survived beyond childhood: Caspar Anton Karl, born in 1774, and Nikolaus Johann, born in 1776.

Johann was far from an ideal father. He was given to drink and to resultant rages, and his problems worsened with age. Yet the musician in him enabled him to observe talent in the young Ludwig. With the stories about the prodigious Wolfgang Amadeus Mozart fresh in his mind, he hoped for the same kind of triumph from his own son. He arranged a public performance for Ludwig at the age of six— although Johann billed him as four—at which the boy showed his prowess at the keyboard and as the author of simple tunes. It made little impression; memories of the child Mozart still lingered, presenting a daunting challenge. There are stories about Johann, returning home after a night of drunken carousing, dragging the six-year-old Ludwig from bed, and forcing him to perform at the keyboard until dawn.

Some bits of information are at hand concerning Ludwig's childhood—not the exquisite documentation of the early days of Mozart, born fourteen years before, but enough to give some clues as to the distinctive figure Ludwig was to cut later in life. A report from his elementary school describes him as "a shy and taciturn boy, observing more and pondering more than he spoke." He was known to be unkempt in appearance, incapable of comprehending the simplest mathematics, a failure in spelling in all languages, a fair hand at penmanship (although that mastery proved fleeting) but an avid reader. Physically clumsy from boyhood, he never learned to dance in time. According to his later friend and biographer Ferdinand Ries, "he could never take anything in his hands without dropping and breaking it. No piece of furniture was safe from him. He frequently knocked his ink pot into the piano."

Somehow, this unpromising blunderer survived. After the age of eleven, he received no formal schooling except for his music lessons. At fourteen, he had his first official job, as assistant organist in the electoral chapel where his father worked. The chief organist, Christian Gottlob Neefe, was one of the first musicians outside the Beethoven family circle to recognize the boy's singular if unruly talent and put him through a rigorous systematic course in the essentials of composition, including a thorough immersion in the preludes and fugues of Bach's *Well-Tempered Clavier*. It was through Neefe, as Beethoven later freely acknowledged, that word of his youthful prowess began to reach the outside world. In an article in *Cramer's Magazine*, dated 2 March 1783, Neefe described the "eleven [actually twelve] -year old" as a "boy of most promising talent… He would surely become a second Wolfgang Amadeus Mozart were he to continue as he has begun."

Yet Ludwig was hardly a prodigy in Mozartian terms; one can only speculate on the talents he might have demonstrated given a more benevolent home atmosphere. The music from the Bonn years is certainly agreeable, but it proves only that its composer had assimilated all the "correct" compositional methods of the day and had only barely begun to move past those clichés toward a language of his own. There is an *E-flat major Piano Concerto* from 1784; its original orchestral parts were lost and it has been reconstructed from the surviving piano score: an agreeable piece with a tender-hearted slow **movement,** such as any of a thousand solid craftsmen of the time might have created. There is more interest in a set of *Piano Quartets* from 1785 which could, in fact, be the first surviving examples of **chamber music** for a piano and three strings. (The two works by Mozart came a few months later.) In two of these works, there are extended melodic episodes which Beethoven would re-employ a few years later, in two of the *Piano Sonatas* published as his *Opus Two.* The masterpiece—relatively speaking—of Beethoven's Bonn years was an extended cantata, composed in 1789 to memorialize the death of the Emperor Joseph II; a setting of a rather lugubrious series of poetic howlings, it was surprisingly effective in its own way. One poem, a vision of a better world to come, warmed "by the sun with its divine rays," drew from Beethoven a noble, serene **melody** that would later appear,

A room in the Beethoven house in Bonn, with the family spinet against one wall.

note for note, at the emotional climax of the **opera** *Fidelio*, as the faithful wife Leonora unlocks the chains of her wrongly imprisoned Florestan. The beauty of this moment, surely, is what keeps this otherwise hidebound, hour-long cantata in the repertory.

The teen-age Beethoven composed furiously and prolifically. A second cantata, in early 1790, celebrated the coronation of Joseph's successor, Leopold II; one choral moment contains a distinct if distant prophecy of some of the choral writing in the finale of the *Ninth Symphony*, thirty-five years in the future. The songs of those early years include a rather melancholy item called *On the Death of a Water Spaniel* and, more important, sketches for a setting of Johann Christoph Friedrich von Schiller's ode *To Joy*, the poem which would become Beethoven's lingering obsession until it achieved fruition in the aforementioned *Ninth*.

As his youthful compositions—and, above all, his phenomenal abilities as a piano virtuoso and master of on-the-spot improvisations—became known in Bonn's musical circles, it became clear that Beethoven's destiny lay far beyond this provincial municipality. Vienna, the center of everything important in music, beckoned, and the seventeen-year-old Ludwig made the journey there to seek his fortune. He was well received by friends of the Bonn aristocrats and got to play for Mozart, who was then at the height of his fame.

The Honor Roll

Despite his social clumsiness, Beethoven was a skilled hand in his choice of dedicatees for his major works. Dedicating a symphony to a past, present, or prospective patron has its counterpart today in the naming of destroyers or concert halls.

❖ Baron Gottfried van Swieten (*Symphony No. 1*) was, among other things, a brilliant musicologist. He had introduced both Mozart and Haydn to the music of Bach, through his collection of manuscripts and through the concerts he produced in his own home.

❖ Prince Carl von Lichnowsky (*Symphony No. 2*) had been alerted to Beethoven's imminent arrival in Vienna by friends in Bonn. He took Beethoven into his home as a long-term house guest, and, for several years, paid him a fair stipend just to keep on composing. Friday morning concerts at his home helped introduce the new arrival to Viennese musical society.

❖ Prince Franz Joseph von Lobkowitz (*Symphony No. 3*) presented the first performances of the *Eroica* in his own music room. With his puffy face and merry, youthful eyes, he could have passed for a sybaritic epicure rather than the shrewd connoisseur he actually was.

Mozart, from all reports, was initially unimpressed with Beethoven's playing but changed his tune when it came time for Beethoven to exhibit his abilities as an improviser. Legend has Mozart predicting that "Beethoven will make a great noise in the musical world"—a statement that if not true, at least sounds true.

But the Vienna journey was aborted by news that Beethoven's mother was dying; he hastened home. Johann van Beethoven sank further into drink and despair, and was fired from his church job in

❖ Count Franz von Oppersdorf (*Symphony No. 4*), a friend of Lichnowsky's, maintained his own orchestra at his palace at Oberglogau. Beethoven planned to dedicate the *Fifth Symphony* to him as well, but changed his mind.

Instead, Prince Lobkowitz and Count Andreas Razumovsky shared the dedication of *Symphonies Nos. 5* and *6*. Razumovsky, the Russian ambassador to the Viennese court, was also the dedicatee of Beethoven's *Op. 59* string quartets. He was a man of enormous enthusiasm and taste, whose descendants still rank high in Viennese circles.

❖ Count Moritz von Fries (*Symphony No. 7*), incomparably wealthy but given to ostentation, also scandalized Viennese society by his dalliance with a French actress.

❖ The *Eighth Symphony* bears no dedication. The "Battle" Symphony was dedicated to England's Prince Regent, later George IV.

❖ Friedrich Wilhelm III of Prussia (*Symphony No. 9*) was known to have walked out midway through one of Beethoven's concerts. Yet Beethoven gave him the *Ninth* "since I enjoy the good fortune, as a citizen of Bonn [which he hadn't seen for over thirty years], to count myself one of your Majesty's subjects."

1787, soon after Maria Magdalena's death. From then on, Ludwig would be the sole means of support for his younger brothers and their ailing father.

He returned to Bonn, and word of his talents spread ever further, especially his talent for taking a tune (one of his own or one suggested from the audience) and spinning it into an improvisation of whatever length suited his fancy. (Most of these improvisations were never captured on paper, but there is an extended piano ramble that did get written down, at the start of a later work, the so-called *Choral Fantasy*.) The local aristocracy invited him into their homes, to play and to teach their children to play the piano; these were the years when the recently invented pianoforte came to be regarded as essential furniture for any family worthy of its cultural pretensions.

His final years in Bonn gave Beethoven, now out of his teens, a gathering of friends who would remain loyal throughout his troubled lifetime. They schooled the young man in literature and poetry, as his former schoolmasters never could; he became a fervent reader of the classics and Shakespeare, before moving on to the eloquent contemporaries, Johann Wolfgang von Goethe and Schiller. It is very likely the new friends were less pleased with Beethoven's fascination with the revolutionary spirit that had lit the torches in North America and in France and now spread across Europe. His friends could polish this rough diamond only so much.

One of his friends was the Count Ferdinand Ernst Waldstein und Wartenberg von Dux, an enlightened nobleman who, being the fourth son of his family, felt no obligation to maintain the aristocratic stance; he was an accomplished pianist, a fair composer, lively and widely cultured. Beethoven's adventurous compositions and improvisations found in Count Waldstein an enthusiastic ear. The two had met at a party in the home of the von Breuning family, whose children Beethoven was teaching. (One of those children, Eleonora, was also reported to be Beethoven's first and purest love interest. She had other plans, however.) Count Waldstein became a firm and valued friend. Knowing Beethoven's poverty, but also his pride, he presented him with sums of money which he always identified as governmental gifts.

In December 1790, Franz Joseph Haydn stopped in Bonn on his way to his phenomenally successful concerts in London. He was feted by the elector. Friends in the city, Count Waldstein probably among them, had tipped him off that the fiery-eyed Ludwig van Beethoven was worth checking out. Haydn looked over the young man's music and heard him play. He then invited Beethoven to come to Vienna, to be his student and to seek his fortune once again in music's capital city. Haydn returned to Vienna in July 1792, after his London conquests, again stopping in Bonn to check up on Beethoven's more recent compositions and to reconfirm his invitation. In November of that year, as the forces of Napoleon's army were pounding their way into the Rhineland, the unruly, young genius from Bonn returned to Vienna and went knocking at Haydn's door. In his pocket was the letter he had received from Count Waldstein at his departure. "Dear Beethoven," it read, "you are going to Vienna in fulfillment of your long-frustrated wishes. The genius of Mozart [who had died in December 1791] is mourning and weeping over the death of her pupil. She found a refuge but no occupation with the inexhaustible Haydn; through him she wishes to form a union with another. With the help of assiduous labor you shall receive Mozart's spirit from Haydn's hands. —Waldstein"

It didn't quite work out that way, but at least Beethoven's life in Vienna had begun. He had, at least temporarily, eluded a confrontation with that other volcanic force of the time, Napoleon Bonaparte. Beethoven never returned to the city of his birth.

Vienna

THE VIENNA OF BEETHOVEN'S TIME was not yet the brilliant international cultural center it would become late in the nineteenth century, when the city was redesigned and the newly laid out Ring encircled everything that was good in life. A start had been made, however. Joseph II, who died in 1789, had created the Augarten on the island between the Danube Canal and the river itself (near today's Prater), "a place for recreation, laid out for all men by their friend." People gathered there in the morning to hear music. Fashionable men and women promenaded; vendors sold oranges and sausages; there were tennis courts, a neo-Greek temple, a parade ground for grenadiers in white uniforms.

Operating at night, in other parts of the city, were concert halls, cafés for piano and song recitals, and theaters. Operas were given at the Theater an der Wien (still thriving) and at the elegant rococo theater at Schönbrunn Palace (also still flourishing). At the homes of the aristocrats, including the palace of the Russian ambassador Prince Andreas Razumovsky, Haydn and Mozart had participated in chamber music performances. Now Mozart was gone, and Haydn had begun to ail, but the music continued. Other palaces competed for the glory of new music: the *Eroica* would have its first hearing (with a drastically reduced orchestra) in the music room of Prince Franz Joseph von Lobkowitz; he and Razumovsky would share the dedication of the *Fifth Symphony.*

Vienna's geographical position greatly enriched its music. Folk music—song and dance—from Budapest and the Balkans flowed to Vienna along the Danube; in Vienna, it mixed with the further riches from Italy and France, and the stern discipline of the Germans. Mozart breathed in this rich mixture and translated it into the most sublime operatic music the world would ever know. Haydn put it into his string quartets. The Italians Domenico Cimarosa and Giovanni Paisiello, and later Gioacchino Antonio Rossini, created comic operas for Vienna of such immediate appeal that they overshadowed the chances of any composer with more serious intent;

Gioacchino Rossini: His comic operas made him far more popular with Vienna's public than Beethoven, yet they were friends, sort of.

Beethoven would soon feel the competition.

Beethoven's path toward Vienna had been greatly smoothed, most of all by the enthusiastic Count Waldstein. Desperate for a "New Mozart"—perhaps even penitent at its neglect of the former one— the Viennese connoisseurs flocked to the first concerts by this disheveled, red-faced new arrival from the Rhineland, listened with awe and delight as he played his first sets of piano sonatas—wildly flailing and mercurial in their mood-shifts—and were astounded with his powers of improvisation.

In the last decade of the eighteenth century, Vienna teemed with competent musical talent; none of it, however, was worthy of receiving the mantle of "New Mozart." Johann Nepomuk Hummel, eight years Beethoven's junior, had been a pupil of Mozart's. Johann Albrechtsberger, who had taken the musical post at the Esterházy court upon Haydn's retirement, was one of the onlookers at Mozart's deathbed, along with the illustrious dilettante and patron Baron Gottfried van Swieten, who had introduced both Haydn and Mozart to the music of Johann Sebastian Bach. These were among the important figures who were already aware of Beethoven's repu-

Antonio Salieri: A highly regarded composer at the Austrian court in Mozart's time, he later became a respected teacher of both Beethoven and Schubert.

tation before his arrival, and who greeted him warmly. So did that political virtuoso and fairish composer Antonio Salieri—"Signor Bonbonieri" as he was jocularly known at court—who by 1792 was firmly ensconced at the head of the Court Orchestra.

In a sense, Beethoven did absorb the essence of the Viennese spirit. He played the game skillfully, played up to the aristocrats who could do him the most good, and turned out small, unimportant piano pieces and dances for aristocratic gatherings. His prowess in sponging off the right people seemed limitless. He arrived in Vienna with a small stipend from Bonn and a further gift to cover his lessons

Luncheon for Ludwig

Bonn, in 1770, was a provincial court city, as responsive to the fashions at the French court as to those of Berlin or Vienna. Beethoven's mother was the daughter of a chief cook at an aristocratic palace; she could have drawn on a fine tradition to feed her family—at least when she could get her husband Johann away from his bottles.

Beethoven's time was also a period of heightened food consciousness throughout Europe, with major texts on gastronomy written by Jean-Anthelme Brillat-Savarin (*The Psychology of Taste,* 1825), and major feats of gastronomy performed by him and Marie-Antoine Carême. By 1792, when Beethoven moved to Vienna, good fare there was ubiquitous; for a small sum, one could obtain a six-course meal, including a choice of seven soups and five kinds of fish. Beethoven probably kept a cook, or tried to. Karl mentions that a certain serving maid "can't cook at all," from which one can infer that culinary ability did not pass unnoticed in the household.

with Haydn. He rented rooms, patronized a wigmaker and a tailor for the first time, and set about informing the city that Ludwig van Beethoven, composer, pianist, and teacher, had arrived and was ready to go to work.

He was also, of course, Ludwig van Beethoven, student; that was, after all, the pretext for his move to Vienna. For all his admiration of the younger man's abilities, however, Haydn was not an ideal teacher. At the age of sixty, he had earned the right to be somewhat lazy in his methods. Furthermore, Beethoven's own rebelliousness merely left Haydn exasperated; sarcastically, he dubbed his pupil "the

For the Austro-Hungarian Empire, Vienna was a melting pot in all respects; writings of the time mention goulash from Hungary, liver from Venice, and Bohemian dumplings. (One can find them all there today, as well.) A meal for Beethoven might have included a pudding or oysters or caviar, for starters; then soup, then the meat course (veal, most likely), followed by the fish course with vegetables, then salad, and, finally, fruit.

Trout was a particular delicacy. The Austrian fisherman's tackle included a watertight keg; upon catching a trout, he placed it carefully into the keg along with water from the stream, thus keeping the fish alive until the moment it was dropped into a pot of simmering stock. There are no words to describe how good this was in Beethoven's time, or today.

Austrians of every class were wine drinkers in Beethoven's day, with a caustic fluid known as *Heurigen* (the new, greenish wine) a springtime favorite. (Not for nothing is there a street leading down from the Grinzing vineyards called "Nausea-Gasse.") A taste for beer developed later in the nineteenth century.

great mogul." Surviving exercise books from their lessons show that Haydn made corrections in forty-two out of 245 musical problems, and that the uncorrected entries contained as many errors as the corrected ones.

The crux of the matter was that Beethoven's take on his musical destiny left little room for outside help or interference. He did begin to see other teachers secretly, studying the rules of **counterpoint** with the pedantic Albrechtsberger, who gloomily prophesied, "He has learned nothing and will never do anything properly." It is also known that Beethoven had studied with Salieri; the two had also become fast friends. These studies were specifically directed at problems of setting Italian texts to music.

By 1794, Beethoven had been taken in as honored house guest by Prince Carl von Lichnowsky, where he was to remain for two years, teaching the children and composing under benevolent circumstances. The set of three *Piano Trios,* published as Beethoven's *Op. 1,* were dedicated in gratitude to the Prince. From such aristocratic support, reinforced by influential friends from Bonn, Beethoven leapfrogged into prominence in the elegant salons of Vienna, bypassing dozens of hopeful virtuoso competitors. Before long, he came to be lionized throughout Central Europe by anyone who was anybody. Above all, he was prized for his improvisations, described by one astounded listener as a "wildly foaming cataract… an utterance so forceful that the stoutest [piano] was scarcely able to withstand it."

Soon he was able to control that "foaming cataract," or at least to temper its force with a **Classical** sense of logic. Already in the first of his *Piano Sonatas*, published as his *Op. 2* and dedicated to Haydn, the great outbursts of ferocity (as in the last movement) are nicely balanced with more rational expression. Perhaps the most successful of these early syntheses came in the *C-minor Piano Sonata, Op. 13*, of 1799, known as the *Pathétique*, a nicely controlled mixture of superheated outcry (e.g., just the opening bars) and just enough pulling-back from time to time to allow the listener to catch a breath.

Within a relatively short time, Beethoven had established himself as a piano virtuoso the equal of any in Europe, and as a composer whose furious and dramatic unorthodoxies were beginning to develop a following—at least among the intellectual liberals of the day. By 1795, his two brothers had come to Vienna from Bonn; their father had died, ending any family connections with their native city. His brothers' proximity stirred Ludwig to heightened ambitions; in February 1796, he set out on a concert tour of Prague, Dresden, and Berlin. In the latter city, he delivered his two *Op. 5 Cello Sonatas* to the cello-mad Friedrich Wilhelm II, King of Prussia, and was rewarded with a gold snuffbox filled with louis d'or. He remained in Berlin for a month and gave frequent demonstrations of his improvisational talents.

Other tours ensued, with Beethoven continually honored for his work at the keyboard and just as ardently rejected by the more frivolous listeners (the Italian comic-opera crowd) for his unruly compositions. A source of further depression came from Haydn, of all people. Returning from London after his second brilliant sojourn there, Haydn had brought back his six final *London Symphonies,* whose extraordinary brilliance inspired in Beethoven (as they should in any composer) feelings of inferiority. He attempted a symphony of his own in 1796, a work in C major, but soon abandoned it as an unworthy competitor. The shock of seeing himself, at least temporarily, as No. 2 had a profound effect on Beethoven, mostly for the better. He no longer composed quickly, letting a work ride to completion on its own store of energy. He began to keep huge sketchbooks and to work laboriously, carving, rejecting, and reworking. (The sketchbooks survive and have been published; they add up to an overpowering study in the compositional process.)

On 2 April 1800, Beethoven presented his first concert for his own benefit, at the Burgtheater. The program included a Mozart symphony and movements from Haydn's *The Creation;* the remainder was all Beethoven: the *Septet* for winds and strings, the *First Symphony,* and either the first or second of his piano **concertos.** The concert was well, but not ecstatically, received; the wind scoring in the *First Symphony,* which falls exquisitely on today's ears, was described as "heavy."

By then, Beethoven's list of published works was considerable: ten piano sonatas, trios for strings and for piano and strings, two piano concertos, six string quartets, and this new symphony. Several publishers were competing for his newest works. Yet, around 1800, he declared that he was not satisfied with anything he had yet created. Adding to this latest bout of insecurity (one of many throughout his lifetime) was the discovery that his health was worsening on several fronts and—above all—that he was gradually losing his hearing, the worst fate that could befall a composer.

Vacationing in the summer of 1802 at the resort at Heiligenstadt, Beethoven composed a letter to his brothers. He never mailed it, but it remained with him for the rest of his life and was found among his papers after his death. It is the writing of a desperate soul, perhaps on the brink of suicide. As doctors had confirmed his hearing loss, he had wanted to die "…but Art, only Art held me back…it seemed impossible to me that I should leave the world before I had produced all I felt I might, and so I spare this wretched life." With an act of heroism echoed in the heroic strains of his greatest music, Beethoven forced himself back to the world of the living. "I shall seize fate by the throat," he later wrote. "Most assuredly it will not get me wholly down."

"I am now making a fresh start," he declared. That "start" was one of the transforming creations in all artistic history, the *Symphony No. 3*, titled *Eroica*. His art had become his means of seizing Fate by the throat; for the remainder of his existence, he never relaxed his grasp.

Storming the Gates

FAR FROM TODAY'S FAMILIAR appraisal as a tyrant and despoiler, Napoleon Bonaparte exerted a strong hold in his own time over the minds of young liberals and other freethinkers. To Beethoven, fascinated as he had always been by the ideals of the French Revolution and disillusioned by the ensuing Reign of Terror, Napoleon appeared as an enlightened liberator of the European masses. Incapable of actually taking up arms in the Napoleonic cause, Beethoven determined, instead, to attach his own music to that cause.

His first two symphonies, full of original touches but still conceived within the framework of a composition by Haydn or Mozart, had been played in Vienna to moderate success. (The *Second Symphony* did, however, elicit the famous description from Vienna's *Newspaper of the Elegant World:* "A crass monster, a hideously wounded dragon that refuses to expire…") Now, however, he was ready to explore new paths. The victorious Napoleon seemed to Beethoven the ideal role model. In 1802, he began to craft a new kind of symphony, one whose design and range of expression went far beyond anything in the repertory of the time: a "heroic" symphony, furthermore, which was to be *about* something. Specifically, it was to be called *Bonaparte*, with the name of that heroic First Consul of France at the top of the title page.

Ferdinand Ries, one of Beethoven's more trustworthy assistants, related in his memoirs what happened next. "I was the first to announce to him the news that Napoleon had declared himself Emperor, whereupon he flew into a rage and cried, 'Then he too is nothing but an ordinary mortal!… Now he will raise himself above all others and become a tyrant!' Beethoven went to the table, took hold of the top of the title page, tore it off and flung it on the ground. This first page was rewritten, and not until then was the symphony entitled 'Sinfonia eroica.'" (Actually, the Ries account, like many other reports from Beethoven's adoring contemporaries, needs some careful editing. The original manuscript of the *Eroica* has never been found; the torn title page—with holes in the paper to memorialize the fury of Beethoven's action—actually exists on a copy made by one of Beethoven's assistants. Napoleon was crowned Emperor in May 1804; as late as October of that year, Beethoven was describing the symphony to a prospective publisher as being dedicated to Bonaparte. In that month, he also jotted down plans to compose a Mass in honor of the French leader. The *Mass,* in C major, was later brought forward as a birthday offering to the wife of another of Vienna's noted patrons, Prince Nikolaus Esterházy.) In any case, the symphony's new dedicatee was the benevolent Prince Lobkowitz, and the first presentation of the work—its heroism somewhat muffled by a drastically pared-down orchestration—was to the Prince's invited guests, late in 1804.

There was no turning back. The *Eroica* had its first public hear-

Napoleon: In this famous painting, he might be posing Bonaparte: posing for a "Heroic" symphony.

ing, this time with its full orchestration, on 7 April 1805; the Viennese critics—at least those whose words have survived—complained in unison at the music's "strangeness" and its inordinate length. For the rest of his life, in fact, Beethoven would reside at the center of a storm of critical controversy; the annals from Vienna, and later from Paris and London, teem with such phrases as "piercing dissonances," "atrocious harmonies," "puny ideas" and the like. "He seems to harbor together doves and crocodiles," one Paris critic chimed in, thereby founding the tradition that exists to the present day, of invoking the animal kingdom as the ultimate symbol of protest against musical progress.

The heroic symphony unleashed a flood of masterpieces to which the epithet might also adhere: the exuberant assertiveness of the "Waldstein" *Piano Sonata* of 1805, dedicated to Beethoven's great Bonn supporter; the deep fury in the companion "Appassionata" *Sonata* of a year later; the set of three string quartets dedicated to Count Razumovsky and first performed at his palace in 1808; the *Fourth Piano Concerto*, by turns elegiac and witty, with its slow movement a clear depiction of a wordless struggle between opposites— Orpheus taming the Furies at the gates of Hades, as Hungarian composer and pianist Franz Liszt later described it. In work after work, Beethoven delighted his admirers and confounded his detractors, as each of these compositions redefined the very essence of the art of music and also defined how much, within that art, an unruly free spirit could get away with.

The range of expression in these middle-period masterpieces is staggering to contemplate. Among the chamber works, the luxuriance and expansiveness of the first "Razumovsky" *Quartet* contrasts strikingly with the fury and the sardonic irony of the second in the series. The serene beauty of the *Violin Concerto* and the *Fourth Symphony* contrast with the wrenching tension, the demonic mutterings, and the ultimate victory celebration of the *Fifth Symphony*; these works, in turn, stand out against the sublime hymns to Nature and the tone-painting that make up the *Sixth*, or *Pastoral Symphony.*

The music burst upon the Viennese public like a series of thunderclaps. Beethoven's friends in high places served him well by orga-

Beethoven as the central figure in a musicale at the elegant home of Count Razumovsky, the music-loving Russian ambassador to Vienna.

nizing a series of "Concerts for Music-Lovers" where, for several years, audiences could sample the latest explosions from his pen. One concert in particular, on 22 December 1808, lingers in the annals of astounding achievements: it included the world premieres of the *Fifth* and *Sixth Symphonies* and the *Fourth Piano Concerto,* parts of the *C-major Mass* and a brand-new choral work written for the occasion, a *Fantasia* involving piano solo, orchestra, and chorus—an event comparable to being present at the creation of the world! Beethoven improvised the solo for the latter work and later wrote down what he had played; it is the best surviving example of his improvisatory style, but to ears that have heard the improv of Charlie Parker, it might sound somewhat tame. More important is the fact that the concluding choral melody is a ringer for the grand hymn-tune-to-come in the finale of the *Ninth Symphony.*

One field of music proved the most difficult to conquer. As long ago as his last years in Bonn, Beethoven had sketched a possible operatic treatment for Johann Wolfgang von Goethe's great *Faust;* despite sporadic exchanges of letters between composer and poet, the project was never really started. In Vienna, he had been approached by Emanuel Schikaneder, still living high on the success of his and Mozart's *Magic Flute* and now in charge of the illustrious Theater an der Wien, with the plan for a "grand heroic opera" to be called *Vesta's Fire,* boasting a cast of characters including Roman soldiers, Vestal virgins, a noble Sabine woman, and a fearsome tangle of plot gimmicks and gestures. Beethoven composed the music for one whole scene before recognizing that the project was dramatically beyond rescue.

Schikaneder's banal verses, he complained, "could only have proceeded from the mouths of our Viennese apple-peddlers." The best of his *Vesta* music then found its way into the next project, Beethoven's only completed opera and the work that caused him the greatest agony.

The list of women in Beethoven's life is voluminous, and the varying natures of the relationships adds up to a sizable catalogue. One woman, however, the Countess Josephine Deym, born of the aristocratic Brunswick (or Brunsvik) family, played a particular role in the formative processes for Beethoven's one completed opera, *Fidelio.* The Countess was widowed in 1804; she and Beethoven began a highly emotional correspondence which lasted until 1807.

She was obviously devoted to him, but she kept him at bay, partly out of loyalty to her recently deceased husband. Nothing came of the relationship; she remarried in 1810. But Josephine's steadfastness seems to have stirred Beethoven deeply, and he transferred his admiration for her to the character of Leonora in his opera—the sturdy wife who takes the name of the boy Fidelio, seeks employment in the prison where her husband has been jailed by a political enemy, and ultimately secures his release and the enemy's downfall.

The genesis of *Fidelio* was a French play, J. N. Bouilly's *Léonore, or Wifely Love*; it had been set as an opera already at least three times—by Pierre Gaveau in Paris in 1798, Fernando Paër in Dresden in 1804, and Simone Mayr in Padua in early 1805. These versions all bore the name *Léonore* or *Leonora;* in deference to their composers, Viennese authorities insisted that Beethoven use the alternative title *Fidelio.*

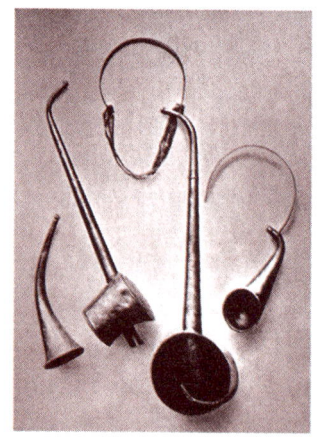

Joseph Sonnleithner prepared a libretto, expanding the original story to include quite a lot of lighthearted byplay between minor characters, the jailer's daughter Marzelline, and his turnkey Jacquino. This proved to be one of several misjudgments that led

Hearing aids and spectacles: Beethoven constantly tried and rejected an array of gadgetry to improve his hearing, to no avail.

Karl Czerny: Even today, his technical studies still terrorize young pianists; he gave the premiere of the "Emperor" concerto, despite what the movie says.

to the opera's failure at its premiere, on 20 November 1805. It did not help, furthermore, that Vienna had fallen to Napoleon only a few days before and that the theater was filled with French soldiers, rather than Beethoven's rightful supporters, on opening night. The opera ran for only three nights, was then withdrawn for revisions, presented again a year later, failed once more, and was then put aside for much-needed and extensive repairs. It wouldn't be until 1814 that *Fidelio*, totally reshaped and even rewritten, would assume the place in the repertory that it enjoys today.

The *Fidelio* fiasco aside, Beethoven's fortunes continued to rise, as the list of masterpieces grew. He lived well. Prince Lichnowsky had guaranteed him a yearly stipend almost from the time of his arrival in Vienna. Almost every work saw publication as soon as the ink was dry. In 1809, several Viennese aristocrats, led by the Archduke Rudolph, formulated an annuity for the composer: 4,000 florins a year, with the stipulation that he remain in Austria. For his benefice the Archduke received his share of lasting fame, as the dedicatee of the "Emperor" *Piano Concerto*, the brilliant piano sonata subtitled *Les adieux* (a kind of tone-poem for piano), the extraordinary sonata known as *Hammerklavier* (designed to test and to challenge the capabilities of a state-of-the-art piano of the time), and, perhaps most important, the great, expansive *Piano Trio* known forever as "The Archduke."

In these years, Beethoven continued the losing struggle against his physical complaints, above all the ongoing advancement of his deafness. Still, he was able to attend a performance of Haydn's *The*

Beethoven and Goethe

The two most influential creative minds of their era were thoroughly immersed in each other's works, exchanged correspondence many times, could have crossed paths several times, but actually met only once. Goethe's first publication of his greatest work, *Faust, a Fragment,* appeared in 1790; still in Bonn, Beethoven sketched a setting of the "Song of the Flea" from that work. No one knows for sure when Goethe first came across Beethoven's music: perhaps in orchestral concerts at Weimar, per-

haps in chamber performances there, perhaps only in newspaper accounts in Leipzig's *Allgemeine musikalische Zeitung,* which Goethe regularly read.

In 1809, Beethoven completed his most extensive Goethe "collaboration," the set of incidental pieces to the heroic drama *Egmont.* Two years before, however, he was still tinkering with plans for something even grander, an opera based on *Faust.* The *Stuttgart Morgenblatt* reported that "the ingenious Beethoven has the concept of composing Goethe's 'Faust,' but so far has found no one who can adapt it. . . We may be certain

Creation given for the composer's seventy-sixth birthday. Afterwards, he fell upon his knees before the elderly, ailing composer and fervently kissed his forehead and hands; the old pitched battles between the rebellious young Beethoven and his most illustrious teacher were now forgotten. But Beethoven's career as a public virtuoso became more and more a trial: he had to forego the chance to introduce the "Emperor" *Concerto* himself; the virtuoso Karl Czerny, whose zillions of practice pieces are known to all hopeful piano students, gave the work its first Vienna performance.

that a deep and truly sensitive product will result [if the opera ever happens]."

It never did. Beethoven wrote to Goethe in 1809, sending the completed *Egmont* score and also proposing the idea of a *Faust* collaboration. It is also likely that the subject was discussed the one time the two actually met, in Teplitz in the summer of 1812. Goethe's reaction to that meeting was less than enthusiastic, however; he found Beethoven's misanthropy "by no means wrong. . . but it certainly does not make the world more enjoyable for himself or for others."

Another significant clue to Goethe's attitude toward Beethoven's music came in 1830, when the young Felix Mendelssohn played him the piano version of the first movement of the *Fifth Symphony*. "That moves one not at all," the poet remarked. "It merely astonishes one; it is merely grandiose. It is tremendous, quite mad; one could fear the whole house might collapse. Imagine the whole lot of them, the entire orchestra, playing it together!"

So much for *Faust*.

Beethoven grew increasingly crotchety as attacks of ill health became more frequent, and they also led to sporadic fallow periods in compositional activity: the year 1811, for example, saw the completion of only a few potboiler orchestral pieces (incidental music to unimportant plays like *The Ruins of Athens* and *King Stefan*). That summer, on a physician's advice, he visited a famous spa at Teplitz in Bohemia, took the waters, and returned sufficiently refreshed to produce two more great symphonies: the Dionysiac *Seventh* (dubbed, not inappropriately, *Apotheosis of the Dance*) and the *Eighth*, a skillfully cut diamond of a piece that seemed to revisit the Classical era and map out a reconciliation with its own time. In his negotiations for the publication of those works, Beethoven had mentioned plans for a third symphony as well, a work in D minor. Whether or not his plans also included incorporating into that work a chorus affirming a great Schiller text on the subject of joy, it would be another twelve years before the proposed *D-minor Symphony* crystallized into reality.

Beethoven returned to Teplitz a year later, in July 1812, this time to pay a call on Johann Wolfgang von Goethe, the enkindling spirit of **enlightenment.** From reports by the two men, it was not an altogether happy encounter. Beethoven seemed shocked at Goethe's willingness to kowtow to mere social superiors. Goethe's reaction to Beethoven was more directly expressed. "His talent amazed me but he is an utterly untamed personality," he wrote in a letter to a friend, "who is not altogether in the wrong in holding the world to be detestable… He is much to be pitied, on the other hand, as his hearing is leaving him, which perhaps mars the musical part of his nature less than the social."

The ensuing years were full of hardships: the passing of some of Beethoven's dearest and most valuable patrons; the destruction of Vienna's economy following the ravages wrought by Napoleonic bombardments and occupation; the passing of Beethoven's brother Caspar Carl and the start of the terrible matter of the guardianship of his son Karl, Beethoven's nephew. It was also the time of the most fascinating of all Beethovenian mysteries, the one which will probably never be solved, though it is perpetually argued: the matter of the Immortal Beloved.

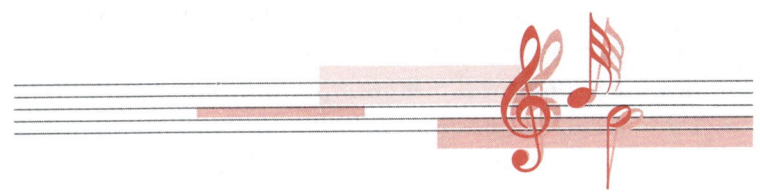

The Private Beethoven

LIKE SOME GRAND PROCESSION by a romantic *corps de ballet,* a stream of women passed through Beethoven's life, from the early years at Bonn to the pain-racked twilight of his life. According to Beethoven's letters and the diary entries of his friends and associates, some new kind of pain was associated with each of these amorous encounters, as they grew, receded, or ultimately disappeared into distant shadows. There is a wonderful if apocryphal scene in one of the first movies about Beethoven, this one by the mystical French director Abel Gance, with the great Harry Baur as the composer. He has been jilted by one of his love interests; he comes to her wedding and sneaks into the organ loft. Suddenly the church is inundated with the thunderous funeral march of the *A-flat Piano Sonata, Op. 26;* revenge is sweet! Nothing of the sort ever happened, so far as is known, but the scene illustrates the attitude

Ludwig at 21: The young man at the end of his childhood days in Bonn, about to set forth to conquer Vienna. From a miniature by Gerhard von Kügelgen.

that undermined virtually all of Beethoven's amorous history: a passion for carrying on impossible quests, an obsession for dominating the scene even when failure looms.

Still in his teens in Bonn, Beethoven was well treated by the von Breuning family. He taught piano to the children, was regarded by Stephan von Breuning as one of the family, and fell tenderly in love with daughter Eleonora. They exchanged letters and gave each other pet names; their written billings and cooings suggest a stereotypically proper eighteenth-century courtship. The Breunings eventually moved to Vienna, in the exodus from the Rhineland that followed Napoleon's invasion. If the two lovebirds resumed their relationship, it couldn't have been for long. Shortly thereafter, Eleonora married Beethoven's friend Franz Gerhard Wegeler, and the couple moved to Koblenz. The Wegelers' friendship with Beethoven continued, however; it was to Franz that Beethoven first confided the news of his deafness. It is unlikely that Beethoven would have performed a funeral march at the wedding of such good friends.

He might have, however, at the nuptials of the Countess Giulietta Guicciardi. Franz Wegeler, during his time in Vienna, had

noted that Beethoven "was always in love" but that his hopes for conquest were of the sort that "an Adonis might have found difficult if
not impossible." A proposal to the singer Magdalena Willmann was
refused; she found him "ugly and half-crazy." And then there was
Giulietta, "a dear charming girl who loves me and whom I love," as
Beethoven described her to Wegeler. Their relationship was memo-
rialized not in bed, but in the dedication to her of the "Moonlight"
Sonata, a love letter at the start which became washed out at the end
by torrential storms. The romance with Giulietta followed a familiar
course; after toying with him for a time, she delivered the ultimate
insult by marrying a far lesser composer, a nonentity named Count
Wenzel Robert Gallenberg.

Giulietta had two cousins, the young Countesses Therese and
Josephine from the aristocratic Brunsvik (or Brunswick) family from
Hungary. They both became Beethoven's piano students in 1799, and
he wrote a charming four-hand duet for them. He was particularly
attached to Josephine and believed there might be hope for a successful courtship when her elderly husband, Count Joseph Deym, left her
a widow in 1804. Beethoven pursued her for three years through the
mail, ardently proposing marriage time after time. It was not to be,
however; Josephine's family declared that the act would violate the
memory of her recently deceased husband, and they seem to have had
no use for Beethoven in any case. At least the steadfast Josephine ultimately did Beethoven some good; she became the inspiration for the
loyal Leonora in *Fidelio*.

True enough: as a lover, Beethoven cut a poor figure. He was undersized and dumpy with a pockmarked, reddish brown face (which resulted in his being known in some circles as "the Black Spaniard"), a mop of wiry dark hair, fiery black eyes, and a chin with a double dimple. The sight of him inspired women to tease and to ridicule his amorous advances.

Yet there was one more woman in his life who can be identified by name and whom, as he proclaimed in 1810, he desired to be his wife—again to no avail. She was Therese Malfatti, and she happened to be the daughter of Beethoven's chief physician. Their grotesque love-games—now hot, now cold, now enchanted, now destroyed by one of her cruel jokes—eventually angered not only Beethoven but also the loyal friends who worried constantly about his propensity for throwing stones in his own path. (Their affair also incensed Therese's father, to the point that, seventeen years later when Beethoven lay dying, he refused to come at first and then delayed his arrival so flagrantly that he might very well have hastened the moment of death.) To

Beethoven at 45, in a more dyspeptic portrait by Christoph Heckel.

soothe the capricious Therese, Beethoven resorted to desperate means. He implored her to continue her music making: "You have such a pretty talent for it," he urged. He sent her a theme for her edification and begged her to study it for once "without the aid of punch." Nothing worked; on Beethoven's part, at least, common sense finally took hold, and he eventually dropped the amorous pursuit.

And then there was the woman who cannot be named, whose mystery-shrouded figure has driven historians and romancers to fantastic heights. A letter, found in Beethoven's papers after his death, is addressed to someone named only as "my immortal beloved" ("unsterbliche Geliebte"): a letter written in three spurts over a twenty-four-hour period—the morning of Monday, 6 July, that evening, and the morning of 7 July. What year? Biographers have struggled with even that basic fact; there were five possible years during the period in question in which 6 July fell on a Monday. To whom? Giulietta? One of the Brunsvik countesses? Many theories as to both date and intended recipients motivated writers throughout the nineteenth century until one historian in 1909, sifting through the evidence with a care not previously exercised, resolved the first question and proved beyond doubt that the letter was written in Teplitz during Beethoven's visit there in 1812, the time of his encounter with Goethe.

The second question, however, lingers without a definitive answer. Who was there in 1812 whom Beethoven could address as "my angel, my all, my very self," assert that "our love is truly founded in heaven," and exhort to "continue to love me, never misjudge your lover's most faithful heart"? Scholars are still at the fascinating task of piecing together circumstantial evidence. All that is known for sure is that whoever the "immortal beloved" might be, she never received the letter. Like the "Heiligenstadt Testament," Beethoven's document of renunciation and affirmation that was addressed to his brothers at the discovery of his deafness, the missive was never sent; it remained among Beethoven's papers, to baffle the world after its writer could no longer be queried. The name of Antonie Brentano, of the famous lit-

Johann von Goethe: Great poet and dramatist, exemplar of the spirit of the Enlightenment, he admired Beethoven, but with trepidation.

erary family, has been advanced, a woman whose purity and intellect Beethoven is known to have admired. But Antonie was married in 1812 and had a small daughter who took piano lessons from Beethoven. True, she was estranged from her husband in and around 1812, and it's also known that Beethoven went from Teplitz, a week or two after the date on the letter, to spend time with the Brentano family at Karlsbad. But the highly moral Beethoven had presented his opinion, on several occasions in several letters, that extramarital lovemaking was an abomination. He had exerted his powers as elder brother—in vain, as it turned out—to break up a relationship between the younger of his two brothers, Nikolaus Johann, and his housekeeper.

The likelihoods do accumulate! Amalie Sebald is a lesser possibility, a charming young singer whose girlish appeal had enchanted Beethoven when they first met the year before. And the list of aspirants to the title of "unsterbliche Geliebte" runs on. Could the participants from two unhappy bygone affairs be considered—the sharp-tongued Magdalena Willmann? Therese Malfatti, the terrible

The Tagebuch

From 1812 to 1818, Beethoven kept a daily diary (*Tagebuch*) which he used as a repository for a wide variety of subjects: a ledger for his financial dealings, a scrapbook of the writings by others that came to his attention, a platform for his own outcries. After Beethoven's death, the book, along with other important documents, passed through many hands, landing finally with his nephew Karl. After Karl's death in 1858, his widow Caroline sold or otherwise disposed of much of the material. The original *Tagebuch* has never turned up; it survives only in several copies that now reside in German museums. Here is a random selection of lines; most of them are undated.

‖ Deepest submission to your fate, only this can give you the sacrifices. . . O hard struggle! (1812)

‖ Learn to keep silent, O friend. Speech is like silver, but to be silent at the right moment is pure gold. (1813)

‖ Stock up on everything in order to control the cheating of xx. Ask x about lights; wrote to x about x.

‖ For example, the diagnosis of the doctors about my life. If recovery is no longer possible, then I must use—??? (1814)

tease? Not likely; whatever his infatuation, Beethoven surely realized that neither of these figures was worthy of the high-flown poetic sentiments that resound (along with banal complaints about the state of his health) throughout this enigmatic three-part letter.

In any case, what little is known of the amorous Beethoven, in the years following the famous letter, comes together in an unattractive patchwork. From 1812 to 1818, he kept a voluminous *Tagebuch*, a daily diary, which he packed with memoranda and meditations on the state of the world, of art, and of God, along with reports of his

❚❚ Shoe brushes for polishing when somebody visits.

❚❚ There is much to be done on earth, do it soon!

❚❚ No time passes more quickly…than when I spend it with my Muse.

❚❚ Never outwardly show people the contempt they deserve, because one cannot know when one may need them.

❚❚ 34 bottles from Countess Erdödy. 15 bottles in the maid's room. 18 shirts.

❚❚ Show your power, Fate! We are not masters of ourselves; what has been decided must be, and so be it! (1816)

❚❚How stupidity and misery remain forever paired. (1818)

❚❚ It would have been impossible without hurting the widow's feelings, but it was not to be. And Thou, almighty God, seest into my heart. Know that I have disregarded my own welfare for my dear Karl's sake, bless the work, bless the widow. Why cannot I entirely follow my heart and henceforth— the widow— (1818)

❚❚ Lamentable Fate, why can I not help you? (1818)

❚❚ In Mödling the new housekeeper started on 8 June 1818.

practical dealings with the outside world. He wrote often about his "state of mental confusion" and even referred obliquely to the "Immortal Beloved": "O terrible circumstances, which do not suppress my longing for domesticity… O God, God, look down on the unhappy Beethoven and do not let it continue." A depressing number of entries deal with prostitutes, "those rotten fortresses," and there is a rueful self-exculpatory note that suggests that he had, indeed, sampled their favors: "the weaknesses of nature are given by nature itself." For a time after 1812, his health worsened; for several months into 1813, he produced virtually nothing of musical importance.

There was, however, one more emotional crisis to deal with, a long-lasting and unpleasant one which threatened more than once to destroy what little remained of Beethoven's health and peace of mind. Caspar Carl, the elder of Ludwig's two younger brothers, had married in 1806; his wife, Johanna, was pregnant at the time. Beethoven made several notations of his disapproval, although relations between him and Caspar Carl had apparently steadied themselves by 1809, when Ludwig sought refuge in his brother's house against the bombardment of Napoleon's troops.

Caspar Carl died in 1815, leaving his widow and his nine-year-old son Karl. His will stipulated a joint guardianship between Ludwig and Johanna. "Inasmuch as the best of harmony does not exist between my brother and my wife… I by no means desire that my son be taken away from his mother." Perhaps remembering Johanna's condition at the time of her marriage, perhaps for any number of other motivations that have been speculated upon for nearly two centuries, Beethoven determined that he and he alone should be the proper guardian for Karl's upbringing, seeing himself as the Sarastro in Mozart's *Magic Flute*, rescuing a child from the evil machinations of the Queen of the Night (his favorite name for Johanna). With considerable justification, she thought otherwise, and a painful court battle was launched, in which Beethoven finally proved Johanna an unsuitable parent and gained custody.

As Beethoven surely realized, the court decision did not imply that he was a suitable parent. There was no place in his unruly lifestyle for a ten-year-old fatherless child. He placed Karl in a boarding school outside Vienna, with orders that Johanna was not to be granted visiting privileges. From then on, his life was dominated by Karl, for reasons psychiatrists may well debate *ad infinitum*. His longing for companionship, for a child of his own, was surely shaped by his own unhappy childhood, where his only real fathering had come from others

The composer at work in his disarrayed study.

than his real father—the kindly Stephan von Breuning, for example. His antipathy toward Johanna was undoubtedly inspired by jealousy, perhaps guilt, perhaps that convenient analysts' catchall: some latent homosexual tendencies that converted Karl into the latest in the stream of love-objects. The theory has even been advanced that Beethoven was actually, perhaps subconsciously, in love with Johanna and looked upon Karl as some kind of linkage to her.

One thing was certain: whatever genuine feelings of love and paternalism Beethoven felt for his nephew, he was pouring them into a bottomless pit. Karl responded poorly to Ludwig's every act of kindness; his unprepossessing uncle nagged him more than once to catatonic despair. To his credit, Beethoven attempted to pour some music into the boy's rebellious skull, but this proved a slow and discouraging process.

Worse yet, two years after the original court decision, Johanna made another attempt to regain custody of her son, citing the physical and mental damage he was suffering under Ludwig. Something horrible came out during this trial: the discovery that the Beethoven family, all the way back to Johann van Beethoven in Bonn, had falsified its noble status and had no right to use the vaulted "van." Upon release of that piece of news, the case was thrown out of the nobles' courtroom and transferred to the commoners' tribunal.

Two more years of litigation ensued, with the hapless Karl, as one observer put it, "bounced back and forth like a ball." Beethoven finally won his case at the order of the Court of Appeals in July of

1820; in the four years since he first acquired guardianship of his nephew, he had produced virtually nothing of notable musical worth. Karl entered the Polytechnic Institute, where he was a poor student and an extravagant spender of his uncle's money. In May 1826, at the age of twenty, he put a bullet into his head but even made a muddle of this. Interviewed in the hospital, he told authorities that his "imprisonment" in Ludwig's home had brought on the desire to kill himself. The attempt was a crushing blow to Ludwig; he went around, according to friends, "looking like a man of seventy."

In January 1827, Karl entered the army. Ludwig's will made him his sole heir, and he later inherited the fortune of his other uncle, Nikolaus Johann, as well. Karl died in 1858, leaving his widow with five children. One of them was named Ludwig.

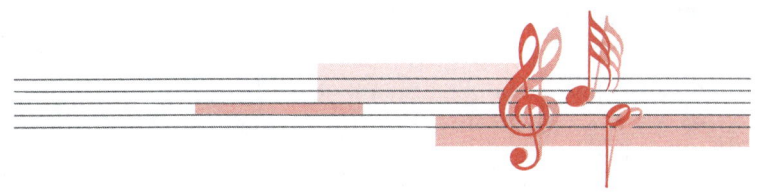

Beethoven's Victory

FOR REASONS POSSIBLY STEMMING from the continuing distress over Karl, from his now virtually total deafness, or from any number of troubles that came to beset Beethoven in the fifth decade of his life, there came a definite slackening in his production of exuberant masterpieces from about 1816 on. The picture wasn't entirely bleak, of course. The opera *Fidelio* had been taken out of mothballs and refurbished with a great deal of new writing and music (including the two glorious arias for Leonora and her imprisoned husband Florestan that are the work's best-known pieces). Now, starting with its born-again premiere in May 1814, this still uneven but stirring music drama achieved its proper recognition. The *Seventh* and *Eighth Symphonies* from 1812 enjoyed continued success, and they were joined by an even more popular work for which Beethoven himself had no great regard:

a *Battle Symphony,* originally composed for a mechanical orchestra, then transcribed for real instruments, consisting mainly of English and French military songs interwoven to represent the Duke of Wellington's victory over Napoleon.

The lack of new orchestral music after these works caused Beethoven's friends some concern. They found the insignificant overtures and incidental pieces (*The Ruins of Athens, King Stefan,* and *Namensfeier*) that trickled forth between 1816 and 1820—the years of the greatest agony over Karl's guardianship—further suggestive of a drying up of the creative torrent. Yet there were compensatory pieces: the huge "Hammerklavier" *Sonata,* celebrating Beethoven's acquisition of a splendid new instrument from the firm of Broadwood in London (but which Beethoven himself could not actually hear) and the serene, ethereal *E-major Sonata.* Beethoven also had begun work on two huge compositions that would come to crown his last years: a solemn *Mass* of majestic proportions, and the *D-minor Symphony* mentioned earlier, but now taking shape as something unprecedented in symphonic annals.

In 1820, with the court case finally closed in his favor, Beethoven seemed to experience a creative rush once again. An entry in his notebook even suggests a relaxation in his hostility toward Karl's mother Johanna: "How it pains me to have to make somebody suffer through my good works for my dear Karl," he wrote, with three exclamation points to underscore his sincerity.

As preparation for his plan to create a grandiose *Missa Solemnis,* to celebrate the elevation of the Archduke Rudolph to Archbishop of Olmütz in 1820, Beethoven applied himself to a thorough examination of music of the past: Gregorian chant, Renaissance counterpoint, and stanzas of the prominent Christian-Catholic hymns. The *Mass* was not completed on time—it was finally produced in 1823—but the studies in old music left their mark on others among Beethoven's final works. The profound slow movement of the *A-minor String Quartet,* for example, was

Beethoven totally bonkers: The image of Beethoven as madman persists today (as in the film Immortal Beloved); *M. Katzaroff's painting bolsters the notion as well.*

composed in the Lydian mode, one of the archaic scales favored in Gregorian chant but later supplanted by the major-minor system. The *B-flat major Quartet* ended with a colossal fugue, obviously inspired by Johann Sebastian Bach, whose *Well-Tempered Clavier* Beethoven had known and played since childhood, but with dissonances that would have sent the Leipzig Kapellmeister up the wall.

Another astonishing work also reflected the practices of past composers, Bach especially. In 1819, the Viennese publisher and sometime composer Anton Diabelli, who had published many of Beethoven's works, cooked up a scheme whereby virtually every active composer in Europe would supply a single variation to a waltz tune of Diabelli's fashioning, and the result would receive grandiose publication as a portfolio of the state of the art at the time. Many composers responded with single entries: among them the twenty-two-year-old Franz Schubert and the eight-year-old Franz Liszt. Beethoven, however, aimed higher. While proclaiming Diabelli's humble tune nothing more than a "cobbler's patch," he transmuted it into not one but thirty-three variations, a work comparable in extent and depth to the *Goldberg Variations* of Bach.

His old friends still came around. Deaf as a post, Beethoven hit upon a scheme for keeping in touch: a "conversation book" in which visitors could "converse" and Beethoven could "answer." Many of the known 400 volumes, alas, were destroyed after Beethoven's death, most likely by unscrupulous biographers seeking to present their subject in the most favorable light. It was in one of the surviving books that a friend inscribed the news that Antonio Salieri, deranged and frothing at the mouth, had tried to cut his throat over his hallucination of having poisoned Mozart.

Beethoven still attempted to participate in chamber music and piano improvisations, and occasionally he even stood on the podium for performances of his music which he could no longer actually hear, let alone conduct. His sonatas and chamber works continued to be performed in Vienna's aristocratic households; although the public at large had succumbed to the seductive strains of the mellifluous comic operas pouring in from Italy, most of them from the prolific pen of Gioacchino Rossini, the circle of cognoscenti around Beethoven's music grew constantly.

In the summer of 1822, he attempted a reconciliation with his one remaining brother, Nikolaus Johann, who had taken Johanna's side in the litigation over Karl, and whose wife Therese he still regarded as something of a whore. "God grant," he wrote to his brother, "that the most natural bond, the bond between brothers, may not again be broken." He took lodgings near his brother's Vienna apartment, but the overture didn't work. Within days, Ludwig and Therese were at each other's throats, and he soon moved out. That summer, too, he received a visit from Rossini himself, thanked him for the delightful *Barber of Seville* and advised him to continue composing in the comic vein and to abandon his more serious operatic manner.

In November 1822, *Fidelio* was revived; its Leonora was the seventeen-year-old Wilhelmine Schröder, who would later create the roles of Senta and Venus for Richard Wagner. Beethoven was to conduct, but at the dress rehearsal he came to realize that the orchestra had broken down completely. Friends urged him to abandon the attempt; he returned home in a state of profound depression.

That was alleviated, however, within a week, by a letter from Prince Nikolas Galitzin (sometimes "Golitsin") of St. Petersburg, inviting Beethoven to compose "one or two string quartets" and to name his own fee. Beethoven accepted eagerly; not "one or two" but three quartets fulfilled the Prince's request. Two further quartets, created for Viennese aristocrats, rounded out a series of chamber works that brought the realm of chamber music to a height of eloquence and introspection that it would never again attain: impassioned, irregular in their observation of structural principles (for example, the work in C-sharp minor, consisting of seven connected movements).

Minority Reports

In their greatest moments the inspiration of both Beethoven and Thoreau express profound truth and deep sentiment, but the intimate passion of it, the storm and stress of it, affected Beethoven in such a way that he could not but be ever showing it, and Thoreau that he could not easily expose it.

Charles Ives

What is Beethoven—whom it is usual to praise unconditionally and to worship as a god—to me? I bow before the greatness of some of his works, but I do not love Beethoven...He has made me tremble, but rather from something like fear. I love the middle period...but I fundamentally detest the last, especially the last quartets. Here there are glimmers, nothing more. The rest is chaos, over which, surrounded by an impenetrable fog, hovers the spirit of this musical Jehovah.

Pyotr Ilich Tchaikovsky

Beethoven and Mozart are sovereign masters, differing one from the other by reason of development in taste. "Genius can, of course, dispense with taste. Of this Beethoven is an example. . ."

Biographer Leon Vallas, quoting Claude Debussy

Beethoven, that plebeian genius, who proudly turned his back on emperors, princes and magnates [!]—that is the Beethoven we love for his unassailable optimism, his virile sadness, for the inspired pathos of his struggle, and for his iron will which enabled him to seize destiny by the throat.

Izvestia, **the Soviet daily, ca. 1936**

The finale of the *A-minor Quartet* in the Galitzin series incorporated music that Beethoven had originally created for a different purpose. It was to serve as the finale for the *D-minor Symphony* that Beethoven had proposed ten years earlier and had been working on, recasting, revising, and rethinking sporadically during the intervening years. Two streams converge: a plan for a setting for chorus, soloists, and orchestra of Friedrich Schiller's *To Joy,* mannered and gesticulative in its language, but thrillingly proclamatory; and a huge and powerful orchestral symphony, at least as long as the *Eroica.* By 1823, the two streams had merged, with the three purely orchestral movements linked to the chorus by a recitative to words by Beethoven himself: "O friends, no longer these tones; let us raise our voices for something even more welcome…"

The momentous concert of 7 May 1824, at the Kärnthnertor Theater where *Fidelio* had recently run, included the premiere of the *Ninth Symphony,* along with several movements from the newly completed *Missa Solemnis.* Rumors had spread that Beethoven, disillusioned by the swing of Viennese taste toward more frivolous fare, had thought to offer the program elsewhere, perhaps Berlin. An open letter from thirty Viennese music-lovers and musicians dissuaded

Beethoven's last piano: A large instrument, gift of the Viennese piano-maker Konrad Graf, capable of accommodating the composer's powerful, late piano works.

him: "…We know that a new flower glows in the garland of your glorious, still unequalled symphonies… Do not longer disappoint the general expectations!"

The concert was ecstatically praised and damned. There had been too little rehearsal time; the cruel vocal counterpoint in the *Missa Solemnis* taxed the chorus; the high notes in the *Ninth Symphony* were beyond the reach of the quartet of soloists, who simply omitted what they could not encompass. Yet the audience erupted in applause after the timpani solos in the scherzo of the symphony, and the ovation at the end was, by all accounts, overpowering. Beethoven heard nothing, neither the disastrous performances nor the ovation; he sat beside the podium, and, at the end, one of the singers turned him around to witness the applause.

Never in his life had Beethoven been confronted with so many offers to create new works; never had he been in worse physical or mental shape to fulfill those offers. The Kärnthnertor Theater's management wanted a new opera; *Macbeth* and *Romeo and Juliet* were among the suggestions. The London Philharmonic Society had offered fifty pounds for a new symphony but had to be content with the first outside-Vienna performance of the *Ninth,* on 21 March 1825.

Nephew Karl had sat in on the negotiations for the London performance; Beethoven still had some hope of transforming the young man into a worthy and useful partner, but that situation continually worsened. Karl had moved out of his uncle's apartment and taken his own quarters; Beethoven wrote letter after letter, some of them barely

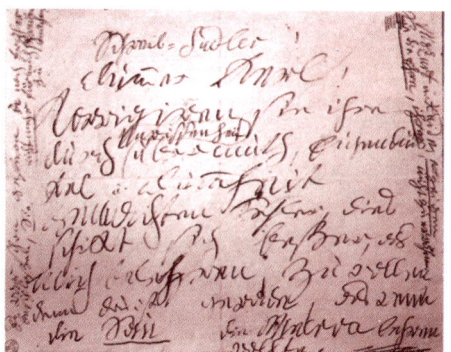

Beethoven anger: In 1825 the copyist Ferdinand Wolanek made the mistake of complaining to Beethoven about his illegible handwriting. Beethoven replied in the margin of Wolanek's letter: "Stupid, conceited ass...You're fired!"

coherent, begging him to return. He even bribed a young musician to spy on Karl and report his activities. These were the pressures that led Karl to his failed suicide attempt, in the summer of 1826. The effect on Beethoven—who, after all, had contemplated but rejected the possibility of suicide as far back as the Heiligenstadt Testament of 1802—was shattering. The disgrace, the ingratitude, the "crime" of suicide was more than he could bear, although it seems never to have occurred to him that he was largely responsible for Karl's action. Upon Karl's eventual recovery, Beethoven used his considerable influence to enlist his nephew in the regiment of Field Marshall Joseph von Stutterheim; in gratitude, he dedicated the *C-sharp minor Quartet* to the probably surprised Field Marshall.

Meanwhile, Beethoven took Karl to his brother Nikolaus Johann's country estate to recuperate from the bullet wound, and once again he made serious attempts to heal the breach with his sister-in-law Therese. He was far from well, but the country air made him nostalgic for his Rhineland birthplace last seen thirty-four years before. He composed one more string quartet, the short and light-weight *F-major,* and a new final movement for the *B-flat major Quartet* in the Galitzin quartets, whose original last movement, a tense and daring fugue lasting nearly a quarter of an hour, had run into protests. (It was published separately as the *Grosse Fuge.*)

Eventually another argument ensued between Ludwig and Nikolaus Johann. On 1 December 1826, Ludwig and Karl left hurriedly for Vienna, in an open coach in freezing weather. Arriving at his Vienna lodgings, after spending a night in an unheated country inn along the way, Beethoven took to his bed with a severe chill. Karl did not take the illness seriously enough to call in a doctor, and most of Beethoven's previous physicians were, in any case, out of town. Finally, a Doctor Andreas Wawruch materialized, who immediately diagnosed pneumonia and initiated treatment.

Nothing really worked. A lifetime of wine and beer had weakened Beethoven's liver, and the weakness had spread throughout his system. His old doctor, Joseph Malfatti, was finally persuaded to forget Beethoven's dalliance with his daughter Therese and showed up. He prescribed the administration of frozen wine punch, which brought temporary relief but further endangerment. By the middle of January 1827, hopes for a cure had vanished.

As news of Beethoven's mortal illness spread, old friends gathered in his rooms at the Schwarzspanierhaus to bid him farewell: performers, publishers, Nikolaus Johann (but not his wife Therese),

Beethoven's one-time pupil and rival Johann Nepomuk Hummel, and another talented young composer, Ferdinand Hiller. Vienna's most promising young composer, Franz Schubert, still fighting for recognition the year before his own death, did not attend, contrary to legend. However, he and his friends followed the progress of the illness with deep concern.

On 23 March, Beethoven took up a pen for the last time, to inscribe a codicil to his will naming Karl and Karl's descendants as his only heirs. The next day, a new shipment of wines, ordered by Dr. Malfatti, arrived at Beethoven's bedside. Beethoven whispered, "Pity, pity, too late!" and fell into a coma. Late in the afternoon of the 26th, during a violent snowfall and thunderstorm, Beethoven momentarily opened his eyes then raised his right hand, clenched into a fist. When his hand fell back, he was dead.

The Viennese crowds that turned out for the funeral on 29 March have been estimated as anywhere from 10,000 to three times that number. The procession wound from Beethoven's home in the Schwarzspanierhaus to the parish cemetery at Währing, where

Oil painting by J. Stieler: Beethoven at 49 (1819).

an eloquent oration by poet Franz Grillparzer was delivered by the actor Heinrich Anschütz. A choir sang a *Miserere* (a psalm of the Bible) to a solemn accompaniment of trombones. Close behind the coffin stood Stephan von Breuning, whose children the master had taught in Bonn, and, for a final reconciliation, Nikolaus Johann and Johanna van Beethoven.

The great composers, with only one exception, continuously rise and fall in the public's esteem; their lives, among music-appreciators, are rising and receding tides of recognition, oblivion, and rediscovery. Beethoven is the one exception. Revered in his lifetime by a relatively small segment of the music-consuming world (while the rest went gaga over the latest tunes from south of the Alpine barrier), his realm grew steadily after his death. One by one the critics of the nineteenth century, and then the twentieth, exerted themselves to find new foaming hyperbole to express the continued power of Beethoven.

To the Romantic imagination, the *Ninth Symphony*, of all the works, spoke in the most congenial language. Even a deaf person knew to honor the work for the heroism of its conception: the consummate gall of a composer to defy the very essence of a symphony by adding words, and to allow the orchestra itself to stage a mighty argument in which the rightness and wrongness of that final music could be debated. There was more to the *Ninth Symphony* than just that final heroism, however. Until its time, a symphony came on strong by announcing what it was to be about, in its clear-cut opening theme in a clear-cut tonality. Beethoven had challenged the idea of stable tonality at the beginning of the *Eroica*, but the start of the *Ninth* went much further. The opening theme seemed to materialize, ever so slowly, out of clouds and thin air.

The idea of beginning a composition in such an indistinct bank of clouds was exactly what the Romantic mind most fancied. Richard Wagner began his mighty *Ring* tetralogy that way: a low orchestral growl that took four minutes just to identify its key, never mind its melodic substance. Anton Bruckner began every one of his symphonies up in a Beethovenian cloud. Richard Strauss' *Also sprach Zarathustra!* took that gambit to its flamboyant outer limit, with results that have been used effectively to sell cheesecake on TV and space travel at the movies.

From the start, Beethoven set about questioning classical practices and then, as it suited his purposes, destroying them. His very first symphony, in many ways beholden to the structural practices of his sometime-teacher Haydn, starts off in the "wrong" key and takes its time coming around. The *Fifth Symphony* shows a unity far beyond the classical concept of contrast; its unmistakable da-da-da-DAAH

Schwarzspanierhaus: The large Vienna apartment where Beethoven died. The funeral service began in its vast courtyard.

motif becomes a ubiquitous binding force (although its presence in the slow movement can be argued); later composers—Franz Liszt being a notable example—used the idea of a composition unified by the recurrence of a single idea, in works for orchestra and in his *B-minor Piano Sonata* as well.

Excerpts from Franz Grillparzer's Funeral Oration

At Beethoven's funeral, 29 March 1827, the Viennese actor Heinrich Anschütz delivered the eulogy, which was written by the popular Austrian poet Franz Grillparzer.

The harp that is hushed! Let me call him so! For he was an artist, and all that was his was his through art alone. The thorns of life had wounded him deeply, and as the castaway clings to the shore, so did he seek refuge in thine arms, O thou glorious sister and peer of the Good and the True, thou balm of wounded hearts, heaven-born Art!. . .

As the rushing behemoth spurns the waves, so did he rove to the uttermost bounds of his art. From the cooing of doves to the rolling of thunder, from the craftiest interweaving of well-weighed expedients of art up to that awful pitch where planful design disappears in the lawless whirl of contending natural forces, he had traversed and grasped it all...

He fled the world because, in the whole range of his loving nature, he found no weapon to oppose it. He withdrew from mankind after he had given them his all and received nothing in return. He dwelt alone, because he found no second Self. But to the end his art beat warm for all men, in fatherly affection for his kindred, for the world his all and his heart's blood.

Thus he was, thus he died, thus he will live to the end of time. . .

(Translation: Oscar Sonneck)

The *Sixth Symphony* practically invents the notion of program music on a symphonic level, with its murmuring brook, its birdcalls, its wonderful thunderstorm, and the hymn of praise when the storm has passed. The slow movement of the *Fourth Piano Concerto,* with

The Autopsy

Beethoven had expressed the wish that the cause of his deafness be investigated. A post-mortem examination was conducted at his home, in the presence of Dr. Andreas Wawruch, his attending physician in his final days. Note: the following descriptions are extremely graphic and should not be read before, during, or after meals.

1) The outer ear was well formed; the auditory canal was covered by scales, which practically concealed the drum. The Eustachian tube was much thickened, and some scars were in evidence. The mastoid cells were lined by a vascular membrane.

2) The facial nerves were unusually thick; the auditory nerves were shriveled, the left one more than the right. The convolutions of the brain were full of water. The dome of the cranium (calvarium) was greatly thickened.

3) The abdominal cavity contained about four quarts of grayish brown fluid. The liver appeared to be shrunk to half its normal size and full of knots the size of beans. The gallbladder contained a dark-brown fluid and an abundance of gravelly sediment. The spleen was double its normal size.

4) The stomach and bowels were greatly distended with air. Both kidneys were covered by a membrane an inch thick, full of brown fluid and also full of stones.

5) The body was much emaciated.

(How could it be otherwise?)

the orchestral menaces, the piano's pleading answers, and the soloist's eventual victory (the singer Orpheus taming the Furies, in other words) is also more than mere abstract musical design. In short, Beethoven conceived of the possibility that wordless music can be *about* something. Composers of ensuing generations saw his achievements as the enabling force for their own innovations.

The music became all things to all people. The earliest surviving recording of a Beethoven symphony, the *Fifth* under the legendary Arthur Nikisch in 1913, would be laughed off any stage today for its gross distortions of tempo, its slowdowns and speedups, its sighing and swooning. But Nikisch himself would be the first to ridicule today's meticulous, controlled, respectful performances—with or without the use of "authentic" instruments—as being somewhat bloodless.

Johann Nepomuk Maelzel, inventor of the panharmonicon, the spring-wound mechanical orchestra that first performed Beethoven's *Battle Symphony,* also created a far more valuable gadget, the metronome. Beethoven used the instrument as a gauge to specify the exact speed for each movement in most of his orchestral works, thus proving his awareness that there would be performances of his music after his death. Some conductors today pride themselves on adherence to Beethoven's metronome markings, ignoring the fact that Beethoven was deaf when he compiled them and, more important, that he was dealing with much smaller orchestras playing in much smaller spaces than today. Other conductors do not, and the arguments rage.

They rage with the other music as well: with the serene poetry of Alfred Brendel's playing of the *Piano Sonatas* as opposed to the headlong impetuousness of the late Glenn Gould; with the lustrous, relaxed playing of the Tokyo String Quartet against the sharper edges in the Alban Berg Quartet's performances.

They will continue to rage. No one has a clue as to the next generation's image of Beethoven and the ideal way to play his music. Will the electronic synthesizer replace the orchestra, as it did in the movie *A Clockwork Orange?* Will the music undergo the romanticized trashing that *Elvira Madigan* inflicted on a Mozart concerto? Or are there hidden depths in the music, inner meanings that the world has yet to discover?

One thing is certain: the music will be around. The eminent critic Michael Steinberg put it as well as anyone. "Beethoven is of all composers," he said, "the one who most insistently tells us that we cannot do without him."

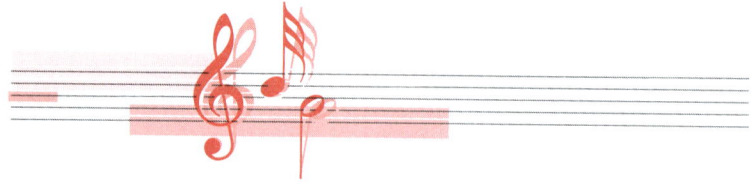

Play by Play:
The Heroic Symphony

"ONE OF THE INCOMPREHENSIBLE DEEDS in arts and letters, the greatest single step made by an individual composer in the history of the symphony and the history of music in general…" The words of the eminent scholar and critic Paul Henry Lang regarding Ludwig van Beethoven's *Third Symphony* go directly to the point. After nearly two centuries, the sheer bravado of the work's conception still succeeds in staggering the imagination.

The power in Beethoven's *Eroica Symphony* has nothing to do with the lore of its origin—Beethoven's early admiration of Napoleon Bonaparte and the disillusionment that led him to cancel the dedication after the charismatic French leader proclaimed himself Emperor. Bonaparte's political cataclysms were summer breezes compared to the upheaval Beethoven's symphony came to represent in the arts. Europe would recover from Napoleon's rampagings; the concept of symphony was forever changed by the *Eroica*.

How?

By 1805, when the *Eroica* had its first public performance, Beethoven had made his reputation as a purveyor of instrumental works structured along more or less orthodox patterns: two symphonies, three piano concertos, chamber music, sonatas. Had he gone no further, his name would still have endured as a composer adept at breathing a certain degree of new freedom into the old, familiar forms, a name to stand alongside the agreeable if hardly revolutionary music of such contemporaries as Johann Nepomuk Hummel and Ludwig Spohr.

The *Pathétique Piano Sonata,* the sublime slow movement of the *Third Piano Concerto,* the wild passions in the *C-minor* and "Kreutzer" *Violin Sonatas*—these were already the intimations of a revolutionary spirit in music. Yet it would have been impossible, even from the evidence of these iconoclastic works, to predict the next turn in Beethoven's road.

What the *Eroica* possessed, above all, was a quality of narrative, a dramatic unfolding that went forward from the first note to the last, that struck an entirely new tone in abstract instrumental music. The classical ideal, brought to its expressive apotheosis in the mature works of Mozart and Haydn, still demanded that a balance be struck; that a work that begins in tragedy—in a minor key, perhaps—must make its peace with some kind of "happy" ending. Thus it was, for example, that Mozart's *Don Giovanni* did not end with the protagonist in the clutches of the demons dragging him down to eternal damnation in the "demonic" key of D minor; there still had to be a resolution, wherein the rest of the cast comes forward and, in a radiant D-major key, solves their own personal problems, prepares to face a Giovanni-less future, and then comes down front to proclaim the moral of the play: that villains are punished and good people rewarded. In the nineteenth century, *Don Giovanni* was the most frequently performed work of Mozart; the Romantics found a kindred spirit in its diabolical overtones. But to preserve that view, most producers omitted that final scene, allowed the opera to end with the Don's violent demise, and thus "freed" the work from the strictures of classicism. Only in this century has *Don Giovanni* been restored to its proper shape.

Mozart had, in his mature piano concertos, developed a kind of writing that invested the soloist and the orchestral instruments with an almost human quality, as if they might be presenting a wordless aria. But Beethoven, without Mozart's matchless ability to turn his sublime, flowing melodies into a semblance of human speech, turned the very momentum of his music into wordless drama. In the *Eroica*, he virtually invented the proposition of musical growth, where the very elements of his language seem to expand, often with explosive force, from one moment to the next. The *Eroica* was the work in which Beethoven first broke completely free of classical constraints.

While paying lip service to the principles that had sustained his predecessors—the idea of four movements of contrasting mood, further contrast through change of key (within each movement, and from one movement to the next), but consistency maintained by a return to the principal key after the contrasting episodes—Beethoven proposed changes in the overall design that were so extreme that only a vast expansion of the traditional symphonic arrangement could contain them. The ideal of balance between opposites becomes secondary to the ideal of constant dramatic impetus. In the magnificent first movement, longer and more complex than any orchestral work previously ventured by any valued composer, an opening theme is only hinted at at the start, and the integrity of the principal key (E-flat) is shattered by a harmonic intrusion within the first ten seconds. Only at the end of the movement (at 16:36) does the listener get to hear that theme as a full-fledged melody; Beethoven has, in those intervening sixteen minutes, swept the music along to that final realization.

Within the first ten bars of the first movement, the battle is joined. Like thousands of pieces before its time, the symphony starts out with two attention-getting chords in the principal key—E-flat, in this case—followed by a theme built out of the notes of the E-flat **arpeggio**—E-flat, G, B-flat—the most direct way of declaring that the work is firmly and resolutely planted in that key. But ten notes into that theme there comes an upheaval: an intruding, dissonant C-sharp which then, by the laws of **harmony,** must be resolved. Within the next few measures, the intruder has been vanquished, and the music resumes its E-flat forward progress. But the shadow of that intrusion remains.

To today's ears, that intruding C-sharp is a small cloud on the horizon; music in the late twentieth century is full of notes that would be considered "wrong" by the rules of classical harmony. To judge the devastating effect of that note in Beethoven's own design, one needs to share the obsessions of the conservative Viennese audience of Beethoven's time, an aristocracy made nervous by the revolutionary outbreaks throughout Europe and the Americas, and threatened by a proletariat impatient to reap the gains that revolution had portended. Napoleon's shadow fell across all of Western Europe; not long after the *Eroica*, the tyrant who had originally inspired it would be at the gates of Vienna, and Beethoven would retire to his cellar with a pillow over his head to blot out the sounds of the invaders' cannon. The invited aristocrats who first heard the *Eroica*, in the music room of the spacious palace of Prince Franz Joseph von Lobkowitz, didn't need any rude, intruding C-sharps to add to their insecurities. Accustomed to the beautiful rationalities of the music of a previous generation—and, for that matter, with the noble Haydn still alive, inactive at seventy-three but honored, nonetheless—many in Beethoven's first audiences heard that dissonance as a monstrous imbalance. (Many, of course, did not. It is one of the truisms of music that the only critical opinions that survive are the ones that go against the verdicts of history.)

That sense of music as ongoing, hurtling narrative is everywhere in the *Eroica*. Listen in the first movement, for example, to the way that same opening half-theme pounds itself into the senses at a point about midway **(T1, 7:04)** and again at **(T1, 7:28):** it sounds first in the lower strings, then is answered by the violins; it repeats and repeats, each time a tone higher; then it splits apart, so that only the first four notes remain. The repetitions come closer and closer; the winds and brass join in. The music wrenches at one's awareness. Listen, also, to those amazing moments (**T1, 2:38** in the first movement, repeated at **T1, 5:52**) when Beethoven delightedly pulls the rug out from under the ongoing three-to-the-bar rhythm, by stressing the "wrong" note and creating the illusion of a shift to two- or four-to-the-bar.

The music seems to revel in its own novelty. "Though the *Eroica* was a portrait of Bonaparte," wrote the eminent musical encyclopedist Sir George Grove, "it is as much a portrait of Beethoven himself." Its genius is the unruly exuberance of a thirty-five-year-old obsessed iconoclast, his peace of mind already undermined by the realization of his growing deafness, his determination firm in not allowing that affliction to slow his pen.

One story, of many, illuminates that determination. There is a famous moment in the first movement of the symphony **(T1, 11:37),** debated in its time and still disturbing today, when the solo horn heralding the return of the principal theme shows up two bars sooner than expected—over the "wrong" harmony, in other words. One of Beethoven's pupils, Ferdinand Ries, relates in his biography of his master that he tried to stop the first rehearsal of the work at that point, rising up in his chair and calling out, "Too soon!" For his mis-directed zeal he was rewarded with a box on the ears from Beethoven and a furious lecture on the sanctity of innovation.

Or take another hair-raising moment, in the slow movement **(T2, 9:24):** a violent, crabbed contrapuntal passage has subsided, and the opening theme of the funeral march has returned—or seems to have, anyhow. But at the highest note in the melody, the music hangs suspended. The orchestra answers with a deep, menacing roar, four octaves down. The strings start a churning motion while the orchestral brass cry out a series of agonized high C's. The orchestra doesn't exactly sing here, as it did in so many of Mozart's sublime slow movements. It shrieks, and that's something new in symphonic annals.

Consider another example, this time in the scherzo. This is the most "regular" of the four movements, following the traditional A-B-A pattern familiar from the minuet movements in the symphonies of Mozart and Haydn but adding a touch of the jocular, even the zany, which led Beethoven to use the term "scherzo" (joke), rather than the polite, courtly dance preferred by his predecessors. At the very end of this relatively brief movement, as the expected literal return of the "A" section dances to its conclusion, Beethoven has a surprise in store **(T3, 4:57):** a sudden change of rhythm in which three-to-the-bar suddenly becomes two—the same trick he had tried several times in the first movement.

"Why?" one might ask. "Why not?" would be Beethoven's likely response.

The finale maintains the sense of innovation. Haydn and Mozart saw their symphonic final movements as a kind of dessert; the heavy thinking occurred in the first two movements, and the tone generally lightened in the last two. (These are, of course, generalizations, which are always dangerous in dealing with the levels of invention in the great works of the Classical era.) It must have been obvious to Beethoven that a brief exercise in frivolity would hardly suffice to balance the awesome expanse of the tremendous first movement and the ensuing funeral march, even with the momentary lightening in the scherzo. His finale, instead, generated yet another grand design: twice as long as any previous symphonic last movement, and more complex as well.

Again, what is most striking here is the music's "narrative" power, the way the foundation for its grand, striding theme is laid, bit by bit, from fragile, tenuous beginnings. The movement itself is remarkably complex and follows no traditional classical structure; at one moment it is a set of variations, at another a capricious attempt to generate a fugue, and, at the climax (T4, 7:50), a peroration of the main theme so grandiose in its scoring that one wants to stand at attention or release white doves bearing flags.

Beethoven always held the *Eroica* as his favorite among his symphonies, even as every subsequent work in that form seemed like a further explosive venture into unexplored territory. His contemporaries were not so sure, however. Beethoven himself conducted the first public performance, on 7 April 1805. "Truly this new work of Beethoven's contains some grand and daring ideas," wrote the critic from the *Allgemeine musikalische Zeitung,* "but the sinfonie would be all the better—it lasts a whole hour—if Beethoven could reconcile himself to make some cuts in it and to bring into the score more light, clarity and unity… Even after several hearings it eludes the most sustained attention, so that the unprepared connoisseur is really shocked. As a result this sinfonie was anything but enjoyed by the greater part of the audience."

Times change.

Symphony No. 3 in E-flat, Op. 55

Scoring: *pairs of flutes, oboes, clarinets, bassoons, trumpets and timpani, three horns, strings. Dedication: Prince Franz Joseph von Lobkowitz. Completed in 1803; first performance (private, with reduced orchestra) in fall 1804; first public performance, 7 April 1805.*

First Movement: *Allegro con brio*

Exposition

Two brusque opening chords demand attention and announce the key of E-flat. The cellos propose a theme (A) using the same notes as those chords, as a quiet, flowing E-flat arpeggio. The flow is interrupted almost immediately, however, **[T1/i1, 0:09]** by an intruding C-sharp that serves as a leading tone, pushing upward to D and then swinging back into the "proper" E-flat context. The intrusion has already taken its toll; that opening arpeggio would, under normal conditions, develop outward to form a full-fledged theme. Actually, Beethoven will withhold that expected resolution until almost the end of this huge movement.

For now, one must be content with only the initial fragment of the theme, which Beethoven will expand upon in breathtaking manner. The winds and the solo horn pick up this fragment **[T1/i1, 0:14]** and move it along, via some upsetting rhythmic transformations at **[T1/i1, 0:29]** and an anticipatory buildup to a grandly scored oration **[T1/i1, 0:46]** for the full orchestra.

> *Note carefully those aforementioned "upsetting rhythmic transformations"; they are Beethoven's way of varying the basic pulse of the music with an ongoing repertory of "surprises" and underscoring the exhilarating sense of propulsion. If the music's basic pulse is 3/4, that means the first of three quarter-notes in each measure receives the strongest emphasis: ONE-two-three, ONE-two-three. If Beethoven chooses to depart from that pattern and lay the stress on some other note, he can alter that sense of regular "three-ishness": ONE-two-THREE, one-TWO-three, ONE-two-THREE; he's hitting hard on every second beat rather than every third, upsetting the music's basic pulse. In this wildly propulsive first movement, it's a device frequently (and thrillingly) employed..*

The grandiose statement dies out almost immediately as a new idea (B) surfaces, little more than a three-note descending figure, echoed among the winds **[T1/i2, 0:56]** and snuffed out by a gruff descending scale-figure. It may be a trivial-sounding theme for now, but one of the Beethovenian miracles is his way of letting small ideas increase in size, like some exotic plant with an overdose of Miracle-Gro. After the descending scale, a large musical paragraph takes shape **[T1/i2, 1:08]**, built out of short, jagged fragments of which one in particular (C) **[T1/i2, 1:21]** bears watching, a dancelike dum-tidi-dum-tidi-dum rushing up and down the scale in the strings. All this furious activity finally reaches a point of repose **[T1/i3, 1:44]** with a new theme (D) of steadier, quieter motion, striking in the way it wavers between major and minor **[T1/i3, 1:55]**. The motion gradually picks up again in a crescendo of activity—an increase of movement, instrumentation, and actual dynamics that sweeps along to a powerful (if brief) new idea (E) **[T1/i3, 2:20]**. This theme whizzes along in a buildup of momentum to the catastrophic moment **[T1/i4, 2:28]** when the rhythm seems to disintegrate into an explosion of cross-purposes (similar to the transformations at 0:29 but even more jagged). This subsides, and a new, soaring theme (F) **[T1/i5, 2:49]** leads to a quick outburst followed by a sort of dying-out reminiscence of theme (A) **[T1/i5, 3:05]** that brings this first section to a close. This swings around, either to a repeat of the entire exposition (minus the two opening, attention-grabbing chords) or toward new horizons.

> *Here is the first major juncture in the classical* **sonata form,** *the end of the exposition wherein the major events of the entire movement are encountered, spread across the tonalities of E-flat (the principal key of*

the entire symphony) and its "dominant" B-flat, the key most closely related. Eighteenth-century practice calls for an exact repeat of the exposition at this point. In the days of the 78-rpm record, when disc space was at a premium, many conductors took the license of ignoring this repeat, which seriously undermined the composer's own conception of the time-scale of the piece. There is no longer a valid excuse (aside from laziness) for this practice. Fortunately, Maestro Solti observes the repeat here. This means that the next 3:14 of the Eroica *will repeat exactly what has just been heard—following the two initial chords. Sit back and listen to the music without a break; or follow the previous analysis by merely adding 3:14 to each timing.*

Development

The sense of fading out in the previous measures continues **[T1/i6, 6:23].** For a moment, the music hangs suspended, rummaging around in various keys, trying to find the "right" one. Remember that the one quality that sets the classical sonata-form development apart from the other sections of the movement (exposition, recapitulation, coda) is this frequent change of key, sometimes via a smooth transition—sometimes, as is often the case with Beethoven, via an explosion.

This development is a fierce, grinding drama. Its participants, at least at the start, are already familiar: bits and pieces from the exposition, sometimes recognizable in their reappearances here, sometimes torn apart into fragments. Leading the pack is the fragmentary theme (B) that didn't promise much at its first appearance (0:56) but now **[T1/i6, 6:49]** holds center stage as its brief, three-note motif journeys through the orchestra. Soon, however, theme (A) intrudes

[T1/i7, 7:04], menacingly scored for low strings and in a minor mode, obsessively repeated—each time at a higher pitch: C to C-sharp to D to G to A to D-flat—and joined from time to time by the dancelike figure (C). The music grows quiet for a moment and the persistent fragmentary theme (B) returns **[T1/i7, 7:56]** but is immediately reduced to a fragment of itself. Now the strings threaten a fugue **[T1/i8, 8:17]** with that fragment as its subject. It has hardly begun, however, when the orchestra decides that the rhythm of that subject (*tum-TAAH-de tum-TAAH-de tum*) is more interesting than its tune. As the rhythmic figure is desperately propounded by the violins **[T1/i8, 8:30],** virtually everybody else in the orchestra sets up a fearsome howl in the same kind of syncopated rhythm that was heard before (2:38). The tension builds; nothing like this had ever taken place in a self-respecting symphony before, and one can well imagine Prince Lobkowitz's party guests looking in anguish for the exit signs. The tension culminates in a violent and prolonged pounding dissonance (an A-minor chord with the brass screaming out an intruding F) **[T1/i8, 8:46]:** unrelated chords smash against one another, the offbeat rhythmic accents persisting, the orchestra at the top of its collective lungs. Once more in his lifetime, Beethoven would pummel his audiences with this kind of calculated savagery: at the start of the last movement of the *Ninth Symphony.* In both cases, the intent seems to be to create a chaos so fearsome as to throw the next music into bold relief.

That is certainly what happens here. As precipitously as the music has roared to this eruption, it suddenly backs away. Out of those murderous chords, the strings sound a retreat **[T1/i9, 9:11]:** four bars of anticipatory throbbing in a key (E minor), unimaginably remote from E-flat, leading to an entirely new tune (G), a plaintive, flowing melody for winds and lower strings, unlike anything previously encountered in this tumultuous movement—a comforting voice from another planet.

Just as suddenly, however, theme (A) pokes its angry countenance into the proceedings **[T1/i9, 9:37],** a kind of "hurry up" reminder that there are sterner matters to be dealt with. But the quiet pleading of the new theme returns once more **[T1/i9, 10:04]** and dissolves into a suspenseful passage **[T1/i9, 10:25]** when everything seems in abeyance for a moment. Hints of (A) sound in the distance **[T1/i9, 10:55],** become more insistent, and then quickly dissolve **[T1/i9, 11:01].** The listener hangs in a void, with a quiet throb on the dominant key of E-flat to suggest that a return to that home key is imminent.

But the suspense is too great for the first horn, which breaks into the sustained harmony two bars "too soon" (by the standards of "normal" phrase-structure) **[T1/i10, 11:37],** creating a rude if short-lived harmonic clash.

This is the moment where, according to the account of Beethoven's disciple Ferdinand Ries, he (Ries) interrupted the rehearsal to scold the horn player for his premature entry, only to receive a box on the ear from Beethoven himself. Beethoven was fond of these overlaps; there's another famous example at the end of the first movement of the well-known Les adieux Piano Sonata. *In Beethoven's time, and for decades after his death, fussy editors strove to "correct" these "rude" passages. Current wisdom, however, leans toward the notion that Beethoven knew what he was doing.*

Recapitulation

Theme (A) returns in the "correct" key of E-flat to celebrate the homecoming. But there is the matter of that intruding C-sharp to contend with, and here **[T1/i10, 11:47]** Beethoven has a delightful new solution. The "intruder" now has transformed from a C-sharp to a D-flat.

> *Those notes are the same on a piano, thanks to the principle of "equal temperament" that came into keyboard music a century before. But they aren't the same for other instruments, and they have the psychological effect on players of "leading" expectations toward the next note—upward for sharps, as from C-sharp to D, downward for flats, as from D-flat to C. And so Beethoven's intruding note from the start of this movement is even trickier than we imagined: a Janus-faced pivotal device that can lead in two opposing directions. There are some corrupt versions of the score, by the way, including one reprinted on the cheap by Dover, that print that D-flat as a C-sharp, probably to remain consistent with the note's earlier appearance. Beethoven's own D-flat is correct, however. In any case, the note behaves like a D-flat, leading downward to C-natural.*

At the point when the recapitulation traditionally reaffirms the initial themes of the movement, and in the original tonality (E-flat, in this case), that intrusive D-flat leads for the moment to another harmonic disturbance, with a rumination through a number of contrasting keys. The horn delivers a soulful version of (A) **[T1/i11, 11:55],** as if to apologize for its ill-timed intrusion eighteen seconds earlier. From here on, however, the music tends to follow the order of events from the exposition—allowing for the fact that Beethoven will want to remain in the same key (E-flat) rather than moving on to B-flat as in the exposition. The full orchestra triumphantly regains its hold on the key E-flat **[T1/i11, 12:22]** with the same triumphant affirmation of (A) as at (0:46). It is in the next few bars, however, that Beethoven makes the sneaky shift that enables him to present the semblance of the events of the exposition without actually losing his grip on E-flat. The corresponding passage in the exposition (0:46-0:56) lasted ten seconds and carried Beethoven from E-flat to B-flat. Now, in a passage lasting twenty-two seconds (12:22-12:44), he emulates Don Quixote's ride by going from here to here while appearing to have gone *there.*

The three-note echoing theme (B) returns **[T1/i11, 12:44=0:56],** followed by the complex of jagged themes **[T1/i11, 12:56=1:08],** including the watched-for dancelike phrase (C) **[T1/i11, 13:09=1:21].** The principal contrasting theme (D) returns **[T1/i12, 13:31=1:44]** orchestrated as before, but in E-flat; the skittering eighth-notes lead once again to the powerful, if brief, theme (E) **[T1/i12, 14:05=2:20]** and to the violent rhythmic upheaval **[T1/i12, 14:25=2:38].** The final brief theme (F) **[T1/i12, 14:36=2:49]** leads to a full close, which immediately tapers off as before [T1/i12, 14:56=3:09] to a remembrance of the opening theme (A).

Coda

The word means "tail," and that also describes the musical function of an extra section optionally tacked on after the principal structural demands of a movement have been fulfilled. In eighteenth-century works, the coda usually served as a brief peroration, sometimes little more than a few additional fanfares to drive home the sense of the music's completion. Beethoven had other ideas. Already in his Second Symphony, *the first movement and finale contain extended perorations that seem to subject the material to one more thorough examination before dismissal. Now, in the first movement of the* Eroica *(and again in the finale), Beethoven comes to regard the coda as an integral part of the movement, where several matters left unresolved now achieve a final resolution. His coda in the first movement lasts almost as long as the exposition and contains at least as many surprises.*

The quiet reminiscence of (A) that closed out the exposition and, again, the recapitulation, now breaks off after the first phrase. It returns [T1/i13, 14:56], but the tone is lower—D-flat (15:04) instead of E-flat. Then, it moves a half-tone lower again—C (15:09) instead of D-flat. Here, at the moment when the self-respecting classical composer should be celebrating the sanctity of his return to the original key, Beethoven has once again upset "normal" expectations and gone wandering. Having thus undermined the stability of his music (and, no doubt, his audience) one more time, Beethoven treats the arrival at the key of C as the chance to swing easily, through several more keys, back to his tonic key (C to F to B-flat to E-flat). Further upsetting the stability, Beethoven now summons up the least expected of the elements in this surprise-laden movement, the plaintive E-minor theme (H) that emerged out of the chaos midway in the development (9:11). Now it returns **[T1/i14, 15:34],** this time in F-minor, drifting off to B-flat minor and then dissolving into a filmy accompaniment figure in the strings **[T1/i14, 15:52].** The lower strings begin the striding motion **[T1/i14, 16:02]** which the sharper-eared listener might recognize as the "suspenseful" passage in the development (10:25); now it leads **[T1/i14, 16:27]** to an entirely new thematic gambit (I). Out of this, the solo horn emerges with something new and wonderful **[T1/i15, 16:36].** Call it the apotheosis of (A), a restatement of the opening theme, but now, for the first time, with an answering phrase that confers upon it a new degree of legitimacy. (Is the solo horn here acting out its contrition for having burst in "prematurely" with the opening theme back at 11:37? No harm in believing so if one wishes!) Under this triumphant horn solo, the strings weave a shimmer of tone, a garland woven out of that dancelike figure (C) that hasn't been heard since (1:08).

The orchestra erupts in delight at this fulfillment of the initial theme **[T1/i15, 16:47],** with a wonderfully insistent *rat-a-tat* from the timpani. It has, after all, taken all this time, sixteen-and-a-half minutes, to resolve the disturbance that wayward C-sharp had caused back at (0:09). There is one final remembrance of (C) **[T1/i15, 17:28],** also a remembrance of those fearsome offbeat accents from (2:28), and a whooshing E-flat arpeggio to bring matters to a breathless close. With two brusque closing E-flat chords, the full orchestra ends the movement the same way it began.

Marcia funebre: Adagio assai

> *The notion of imparting a specific state of mind to a symphonic movement, and giving it a name, is one of Beethoven's extraordinary inventions. He is illustrating here that, beyond the abstract matters of design, unity, and contrast, beyond such technical phenomena as fugue or variations, music can be about something. He had written funeral marches before (i.e., slow music in a minor key and with imitations of muted drum rolls and the sorrowing tread of marchers). There is one in his* Piano Sonata in A-flat, Op. 26, *composed in 1800, and its mournful opening melody is echoed (without, however, the marchlike beat) in the familiar opening movement of the* "Moonlight" Sonata, Op. 27, No. 2, *of a year later. In a set of marches composed in 1803 (two years before the* Eroica*) for piano duet,* Op. 45, *there are passages that imitate the percussion effects that show up in the march in the* Eroica, *but in a much jollier mood. The* "Marcia funebre" *of the* Eroica *is the ancestor of symphonic funeral marches from Beethoven's time on, from Schubert to Mahler and beyond.*

The funereal tune (A) begins on an upbeat that is almost a sob. Under the solemn melody intoned by strings, the double basses growl out an accompanying figure like the roll of muted drums **[T2/i1, 0:00].** A solo oboe takes up the theme **[T2/i1, 0:35]** over sustained chords from the clarinets, oboes, and horns, punctuating soft thumps from the timpani, and the entire string section imitating the throbbing of the muted drums—as they will more than once during this movement. The strings now present a consequent theme (B) **[T2/i2, 1:01]** that actually consists of several jagged fragments. The flowing opening phrase (B1) breaks off for a quick, agonized cry at (1:16), quickly resumes and leads to an even sadder rounding-off (B2) at (1:28). Theme (A) returns **[T2/i2, 1:54]** in the strings as before, its progress impeded by sudden silences and a sense that the theme is breaking apart. Now the (B1+2) sequence repeats **[T2/i2, 2:20],** with the oboe taking the theme and the strings once again recapturing the throbbing, drumlike accompaniment. Theme (A) reappears in the winds **[T2/i2, 3:13],** punctuated by brass and single strokes on the drums. A closing episode presents a new theme, (C), its sense of quiet melancholy almost unbearable **[T2/i2, 3:32],** proposed by the strings and bassoons (a remarkable mix of sonority!) and answered by a stabbing cadence from the full orchestra with the strings once again serving as the muffled drums. This whole first section—think of it as a confrontation between the strings on one side and the full orchestra on the other—has presented a solemn funeral scene in gradually rising intensity. Now that whole complex episode dies off into silence.

Everything changes. From the somber depths of the minor key, the music moves to the blinding brightness of C major, a reminder that Beethoven's original full title for this movement was *Funeral March on the Death of a Hero.* After the funeral march, one must regard the hero. Oboe, flute, and clarinet offer a new theme (D) **[T2/i3, 4:21]** in happy dialogue over a purring C-major accompaniment in the strings, moving to the closely contrasting key of G major and coming to rest with a huge, brassy, punctuating cadence from the full orchestra in that key **[T2/i3, 4:45].** An answering phrase **[T2/i3, 5:02]** seems to evaporate into bright, clear air as a solo flute and the higher strings break the tune apart into airy fragments as they work their way back to C major; then the opening phrase (D) returns **[T2/i3, 5:33],** coming to its full cadence, with the splendor of the orchestra once again deployed.

In a devastating retreat, however, the music collapses back into its C-minor gloom. Four bars from the strings in unison, and a reprise of (A) occurs as originally heard **[T2/i4, 6:26]**—or so it seems. But at the end of the phrase, the music takes a quiet upward leap (6:51) into another closely related key, F minor. Here, the second violins propose something entirely new once again, a melodic fragment that sounds ripe for becoming the subject of a fugue (E) **[T2/i5, 7:02].** It's a terse, rather barren subject, as befits the mood of the music: hardly fit company for, say, the exuberant, dancing fugue in the third of Beethoven's "Razumovsky" *String Quartets* from the same year. In any case, the idea of maintaining the fugal texture doesn't seem to be the order of the day. The low strings enter into the fugal texture **[T2/i5, 7:24],** but not much later the orchestra seems more involved with proclaiming the fugal subject in unison than carrying on the contrapuntal development. Winds and brass proclaim it **[T2/i5, 7:51];** clarinets and the second horn call it forth **[T2/i5, 8:06].** The violins soar up to the stratosphere of their range and sustain a halo of sixteenth-note triplets as the rest of the orchestra shouts forth the fugal theme one last time **[T2/i5, 8:33].** A moment of silence **[T2/i6, 8:53]** and then the first violins, softly and without support, whisper (A) once again, the start of the march theme **[T2/i6, 9:09].** They don't get very far; a timid, high A-flat is answered by the same note four octaves down, in a thunderous roar from cellos and double basses **[T2/i6, 9:24].** In an outburst of grief like nothing before in orchestral annals, the brass players scream out in a series of agonized, repeated Cs resolving finally to F, while the strings churn out an accompaniment in triplets, a bleak, black landscape over which the cries resound.

As suddenly as this extraordinary episode burst out, it now recedes **[T2/i6, 9:59].** The string players' accompaniment triplets are highlighted by the flutes at the top of their range, while the rest of the winds sing a somewhat smoothed-out version of (A) **[T2/i7, 10:15].** The triplets fade away for the moment, as the strings take up theme (B1) **[T2/i7, 10:42],** but then return. The orchestral sonority is gradually enriched, as the strings play their accompaniments in increasingly busy figurations. Quietly, the orchestra remembers theme (B2), elegantly passed from strings to winds, surrounded by accompaniment figures like distant points of light **[T2/i7, 11:08].** The march theme (A) sings out in the winds **[T2/i7, 11:37].** Theme (C) returns in the strings **[T2/i7, 11:56]** and here, for the first time, the "drumrolls," hitherto played by the low strings, are actually taken up by drums.

The miracle of Beethoven—one of them, at any rate—is his mastery of the art of surprise. The listener has experienced this several times already in the Eroica, *from the unexpected C-sharp right at the start, the extraordinary rhythmic fluctuations that make twos sound like threes and vice versa, and the sequence of false starts in "wrong" keys at the start of the coda of the first movement. One of the most striking tricks in his plentiful bag is this matter of the "deceptive cadence." Certain harmonies are stable within a given key; they are heard as self-sufficient. If a piece is in E-flat, say, every E-flat chord will suggest a return to home. Other chords might sound stable if played alone at the piano, but in the context of a piece they demand resolution to an expected, specific, stable chord. If one's ears are full of the sound of, say, E-flat, a chord on B-flat will demand resolution to a chord on E-flat. The constant flow, from instability to stability, from dissonance to resolution, shapes one's subliminal response to tonal music; it is the force that makes music move. But what happens to these responses when Beethoven toys with expectations by resolving that B-flat chord to the "wrong" harmony—a C-minor chord, say, or B major? It's a jolt; not as strong to the ears of today's audience as to Beethoven's 1805 audience, but a jolt nevertheless. This movement is full of these deceptions; the slow pace of the music makes them all the more apparent and poignant. That sudden A-flat at (9:24) is such a dramatic touch, and the one about to happen is no less so.*

Heading for C minor, the music veers instead to a deceptive cadence on A-flat **[T2/i8, 12:28].** A quiet, new theme (F) in A-flat **[T2/i8, 12:44]** leads to a reprise of (B2) **[T2/i8, 13:22]** in the "proper" key of C minor but then to a complete collapse **[T2/i8, 13:34],** as fragments of themes (A) and (B) turn to sand; until **[T2/i8, 14:26],** the strings stammer out bits and pieces of (A), and any sense of ongoing rhythm disappears. Gusts of silence alternate with the fragments;

the orchestra seems so completely undone by grief that it can no longer articulate the entire theme. And the "drumbeats" in the cellos and basses echo from the procession as it files past and vanishes on the horizon.

Third movement: *Scherzo: Allegro vivace*

> *The classical symphony supplied relief, after the serious tone of the first two movements, with something lighter, possibly even dancelike: usually a minuet, with a contrasting section sometimes (but not always) played by three wind instruments and, therefore, traditionally titled "trio." The form of these movements tended to be a simple A-B-A arrangement: minuet-trio-minuet. The first "A" section, furthermore, consisted of two parts, each repeated; on the return of "A," the repeats were traditionally omitted. (Some contemporary conductors dispute this omission and honor the repeats both before and after the trio. That can make for a long evening.)*

> *By 1800, the minuet had gone out of style as a dance at aristocratic gatherings, and out of style, as well, as the traditional "comic relief" in concert music. Haydn had used the term "scherzo" (i.e., "joke") for some of his boisterous movements, and Beethoven took up that term as well, starting with his* Second Symphony. *In the* Eroica, *he goes a step farther, violating the traditional, simple A-B-A pattern with one of his notorious rhythmic surprises right at the end of the final "A." One joke, he reasoned, deserves another.*

Out of a mysterious buzzing, a theme takes shape, proposed by the solo oboe over the throb of strings **[T3/i1, 0:01];** it's not easy to tell, in fact, where the buzzing ends and the theme begins—that's part of

Beethoven's joke. So is the fact, by the way, that although the movement is nominally in the "correct" key of E-flat, Beethoven's theme seems to want to sideslip continually into B-flat, the closely related "dominant" key. The initial sequence repeats **[T3/i1, 0:10]** with flute and bassoon reinforcing the cadence. The buzzing resumes **[T3/i2, 0:16],** but this time it starts to wander through keys: from F (0:22) to G (0:26) to D (0:37) and, via a delicious sudden plop (0:39), to B-flat where the opening sequence (A) resumes in this new key and with more resonant orchestration **[T3/i2, 0:47].** The key of B-flat leads smoothly back to the tonic E-flat **[T3/i2, 0:59],** where a new closing theme (B), built out of the E-flat arpeggio, leads to a dizzying sequence: bits and pieces of the "buzzing" music, set as a dialogue between winds and strings **[T3/i2, 1:05],** and an exhilarating rush **[T3/i2, 1:12]** to a final cadence, with a repeat sign indicating that the entire passage from (0:16) is to be repeated. In something under ninety seconds, Beethoven has zoomed through a magnificently shaped energy field, and left the audience breathless.

The literal repeat **[T3/i3, 1:23-2:32]** brings the "A" section to a close. The contrasting "Trio" is, indeed, what its name suggests: three horns taking on a typically hornlike melody, the sort associated with hunting (or with Siegfried's journey down the Rhine in Richard Wagner's *Ring of the Nibelungen*) **[T3/i4, 2:33].** Bear in mind that Beethoven's horns were played without valves; the player formed the notes entirely with lips against mouthpiece. For these instruments, the arpeggios—the first members of the overtone series—were the

easiest to play, and Beethoven's tune favors those notes. Oboes, clarinets, bassoons, and strings "answer" the horns; the sequence repeats
[T3/i4, 2:40]. Strings and winds lead away from the horns' melody
[T3/i4, 2:49], but these brassbound warriors return **[T3/i4, 3:04],**
their harmonies somewhat enriched to dramatize the final moments
of their stint. This last sequence, from (2:49), is now literally repeated,
but with the harmony darkened at the very end **[T3/i4, 3:23-3:55]** to
build a moment of suspense.

That leads to the almost-literal repeat of the "A" section of the
scherzo. The first theme slyly emerges from the initial buzzing, as
before **[T3/i5, 3:55=0:01].** The music wanders through several keys
[T3/i5, 4:11=0:16]; the closing theme (B) leads to the expected firm
cadence **[T3/i5, 4:53=0:59].** (This section is not, however, repeated
as it had been the first time around.) Now, Beethoven springs his final
joke (for this movement, at least). At the very end, the rhythm
changes; four bars of *alla breve* (counting in twos) interrupt the headlong 3/4 surge **[T3/i6, 4:57]** and just as suddenly vanish—so unex-
pectedly that one hears it in a double-take. The music resumes its regular pattern **[T3/i6, 5:01=1:12].** A brief coda **[T3/i7, 5:17],** full of the
roar of timpani and with the horns providing a final flourish, brings
the movement to a breathless close.

Fourth movement: *Finale: Allegro molto*

The strings initiate the action in a headlong rush, crowned with
the full orchestra at the end, that the ear might want to hear as a con-

tinuation of the energy of the previous movement **[T4/i1, 0:01].** Immediately, however, the sound and motion are throttled down to a minimum **[T4/i1, 0:12],** as the plucked strings (pizzicato) begin to pick out the bare outline (A) of what could either be a theme or merely the harmonic skeleton of a theme. (As will soon be discovered, it turns out to be both.) The winds lend tiny points of color to the second strain **[T4/i1, 0:24],** and the full orchestra briefly voices its approval **[T4/i1, 0:37].** The strings, in turn, echo that approving flourish and finish off the theme, pizzicato, with the discreet help of the winds.

> *Here is the start of a set of variations, although an unusual one. The process of constructing extended compositions out of a string of differing treatments of an original, basic theme goes far back in music history—to the "Divisions on a Ground" of sixteenth-century keyboard and lute composers, to the passacaglias and chaconnes of Baroque masters from Monteverdi to Bach, and to such famous examples as the first movement of Mozart's* Turkish Rondo *sonata and the "Surprise" movement of Haydn's* Surprise Symphony. *Sets of variations, large and small, occupied Beethoven throughout his career. He wrote potboilers on familiar tunes (including the British national anthem); several of his piano sonatas (Op. 14, No. 2; Op. 26, the* Appassionata; *and the* Hammerklavier*) contain slow movements in variation form; so do the* Seventh *and the* Ninth Symphonies. *A separate piano work,* Thirty-Three Variations on a Theme *by* Diabelli, *ranks among the greatest of all ventures in this form. The variation form is not necessarily a cut-and-dried progression from one treatment to the next. In this movement, for example, are two sets of*

variations occurring simultaneously. The first theme has been heard;
soon that will serve as the basis for a whole new theme, and the
remainder of this magnificent movement will consist of a free
alternation of treatments of one theme, the other theme, or both
themes combined. Amazing!

First Variation **[T4/i1, 0:50]:** The theme repeats in the second violins, with the first violins and cellos wreathing it with a flowing countermelody (A2), which will reappear later in the movement. Each half
of the variation is repeated.

Second Variation **[T4/i1, 1:22]:** Violas join the violins and cellos. The first violin takes the theme, while the other strings skitter up
and down with a garrulous accompaniment in triplets. Again, as in
the first variation, each section repeats. But then Beethoven drops the
"formal" structure; from here on, the variation principle is handled
with glorious freedom.

The winds now present the second variation theme (B), **[T4/i2,
1:54]** flowing and insinuating where the first theme (A) was more
skeletal, yet clearly an offshoot of the earlier theme. The woodwinds
sing it, over a running accompaniment of sixteenth-notes in the
strings. But listen carefully; in the lower strings, the horns, and one
of the two bassoons, theme (A) is still at hand, still a skeleton but now
elegantly fleshed out by the new theme. Violins and violas pick up the
tune on the repeat, with the trumpets blaring out theme (A) **[T4/i2,
2:01].** Consider the lavishness of Beethoven's treatment of this new
theme; compare, for example, the point of articulation about three-

quarters of the way through theme (A) (0:40)—three stentorian notes, echoed, one more note, echoed, then a pause (0:32, repeated 0:40)—to the comparable moment in theme (B)—the same three notes, now wreathed in garlands of faster notes from oboe and strings, and the pause made more dramatic (2:13, repeated at 2:22 with even more opulent scoring). It's a most expressive exercise of two musical streams joining harmoniously.

The strings pull away from all that opulence **[T4/i3, 2:28]** with a backward look at theme (B), colored by a touch of minor-key harmony. Now the strings and woodwinds work up a dauntingly complex, if brief, fugue **[T4/i3, 2:54],** based on not one but two elements derived from early in the movement: theme (A) in its skeletal form and the countermelody (A2), encountered at (0:50). Beethoven runs them together in a series of fugal entries, with violins and cellos stating the two parts of the theme at first and the rest of the orchestra joining in. Both theme elements enter in close order **[T4/i3, 3:01]**—oboe first, then clarinet, violins, and bassoon—and lead to a moment's repose at **[T4/i4, 3:27],** with the flutes and violins in a melancholy harmonization of (B), which has, during all this fuss, slipped off to the extremely unrelated key of B minor.

> *A brief discussion of key relationships: the basis of classical structure is the interplay of keys. If two keys share most of the same notes (for example, C major and G major, with the only difference being the F-sharp in G major opposed to the F-natural in C major), they are said to be closely related, and the composer can easily change ("modulate")*

from one to another as a means of obtaining contrast within a composition while preserving some sense of unity. Keys less closely related share fewer notes, and modulating from one to another generally produces some degree of shock. Why is any of this important? One reason is that, especially in the eighteenth and early nineteenth centuries, certain instruments performed better in certain keys; that's why the horns in the scherzo sounded so happy in E-flat major. Trumpets in Beethoven's time were most powerful in C, as in their great outbursts in the funeral march. There are other reasons; aestheticians go on for days about the "personality" of keys— Beethoven's "C-minor style," for example. Most people probably recognize more differences from one key to another than they think they do, especially in the music of Beethoven's time. And it is somewhat unusual to find the key of B minor in the middle of E-flat major; the keys have only two notes in common.

Time, now, for a brief flute concerto; the flute has a fling with theme (B) **[T4/i4, 3:35],** all done up in patterlike figuration, now in the key of D major (a close relative of B minor, but still distant from E-flat). The orchestra gathers momentum and seems to be pushing forward toward new territory. The key shifts to G minor, an easy hop from D and a fairly close relative of both C and E-flat as well. Winds and strings thunder out a new theme (C) **[T4/i5, 4:01]** while, far down below, the cellos and double-basses thunder out theme (A). (The double-basses always sound an octave lower than the written note. Here, however, Beethoven is careful to write the double-bass line an octave higher than the cellos, so that they will come out playing the same note, thus reinforcing the thunder.) The violins and flutes take over theme (A) the second time around **[T4/i5, 4:15],** as this new theme, with its insistent, jagged rhythms, churns ahead.

Flute and violins take up a quieter, gentler version of (B) in the key of C, with the ubiquitous (A) resounding in the lower strings **[T4/i6, 4:43].** Almost immediately, however, the music heads off into another fugue **[T4/i6, 4:52],** with theme (B) in C minor in the second violins and theme (A) bouncing around among the winds and horn. Now the strings take up theme (A) in an upside-down version (a "mirror image" or "inversion") **[T4/i7, 5:02],** and that spins through the string sections while the flute chimes in with a saucy, rhythmically skewed version of (B) **[T4/i6, 5:15];** everything, in other words, has suddenly gone out of shape. But then the orchestra regains its senses. Winds and brass triumphantly proclaim a right-side-up version of (A) **[T4/i6, 5:36],** which resounds at great length through the entire orchestra and sets the stage for something tremendous to take place.

Yes, but what?

The orchestra comes to rest on a resonant cadence on B-flat, setting up an expectation for a return to the principal key of E-flat. The tempo slows to poco andante, and the winds proclaim theme (B) in a richly harmonized, solemn incarnation **[T4/i7, 6:11].** The strings echo with an even richer harmonization **[T4/i7, 6:36].** The orchestra becomes fabulously juicy for the second part of the theme **[T4/i7, 7:02]:** the oboes in a decorated variant, the clarinets in rolling arpeggios (a real Mozartian sound), all against the horns' sustained notes and the strings' figuration. The glorious noise repeats **[T4/i7, 7:28]** in even richer scoring. Finally **[T4/i8, 7:50],** the movement comes to one of the most grandiose perorations in all symphonic music: horns, lower winds, lower strings giving their all to the ultimate splendor of theme (B).

The music subsides, momentarily **[T4/i9, 8:37];** scraps of theme (B) pass back and forth from winds to strings. Clarinet, horn, and violins meditate on just a fragment (three repeated notes) of (B) **[T4/i9, 9:13]** and inflate this into a momentary harmonic crisis. But the music then subsides **[T4/i9, 9:49];** a throbbing in the cellos suggests a slowing down of activity. But no; the movement began with a great whoosh, and so it will end. The tempo quickens; the strings set up a furious thrashing **[T4/i10, 10:22]** as before. This time, however, through it all resounds Beethoven's glorious (B) one more time **[T4/i10, 10:26],** its rhythms altered but recognizable, its triumph unmistakable. The rest is a fabulous fanfare for full orchestra, culminating in a set of pounding E-flat chords **[T4/i10, 10:54]** to round off the challenge that began fifty minutes before. The hero may have died, but heroism survives.

Overture to "Egmont," Op. 84

Scoring: *piccolo; pairs of flutes, oboes, clarinets, bassoons, and trumpets; four horns; timpani; and strings. Completed, in 1809; first performance, 15 June 1810.*

Beethoven's Overture *to his incidental music for Goethe's* Egmont *follows the outline of a sonata-form movement, with slow introduction and coda, that one would find as the first movements of the* Symphonies Nos. 1, 2, 4, *and* 7—*but with some interesting differences that probably relate to the use of this* Overture *in a dramatic context. For one thing, the most identifiable rhythmic figure in the slow introduction returns in the body of the movement to form the second theme. This idea of tying together separate parts of a sonata-form movement in this manner was not yet common; it happens in one or two of Haydn's mature symphonies (*Nos. 98 *and* 103*) and in Beethoven's* Pathétique *and* Tempest *Piano sonatas. In later generations, composers became obsessed with this idea of unifying the content of a movement and breaking away from the formalism of classical structure. Here, for whatever reason, Beethoven is flexing his muscles in that same direction.*

The brilliant coda that bursts in upon the end of the Overture *has no relationship to what has gone before; it is, however, the music that Beethoven will reintroduce in his full set of incidental music, at the end of Goethe's play, a "Symphony of Victory" as the heroic Egmont, who has led his fellow Flemings in a brilliant but unsuccessful uprising against their foreign oppressors, proclaims his courage one last time on his way to the scaffold. In that sense, of course, the entire* Overture *becomes a synopsis of the play itself, much the way Beethoven's third* Leonore Overture *serves as a synopsis of the action in the opera* Fidelio.

A stentorian F sounded by the entire orchestra (minus timpani) **[T5/i1, 0:01]** commands the listener's attention. It is followed immediately by an equally engrossing, pounding, rhythmic figure, which will play an important role throughout the overture **[T5/i1, 0:05].**

"Egmont" Overture: The title page for the incidental music composed by Beethoven for Goethe's play.

From even a sketchy knowledge of Goethe's play, one can surmise that these menacing, heavy, F-minor chords depict the bad guys of the plot, the absentee government of Spain's Duke of Alva which is holding Flanders under its cruel domain.

Just as easily, one can assume that the sad answering theme in the winds **[T5/i1, 0:25]** is the spirit of the enslaved Flanders and, as well, of the heroine of the play, Egmont's beloved Clärchen. That menacing, unharmonized F sounds again **[T5/i1, 0:46],** followed again by the rhythmic figure, somewhat shortened, and the answering figure in the winds. Quietly and menacingly, the lower strings sustain the rhythmic figure **[T5/i1, 1:15],** while above there is a new, pathetic theme, revealed in dialogue between strings, lower woodwinds, and the flute. This all fades back to a moment of silent suspense.

That new dialogue theme increases in speed and intensity, ushering in the main part of the *Overture* **[T5/i2, 2:02].** A fresh theme seems to break into two parts, both tinged with tragedy: the first (A) smooth-flowing in quarter notes, the second (B) marked by a distinctive figure in eighths. The two parts of the theme repeat somewhat more forcefully **[T5/i2, 2:37]** and come to a full close at (2:55).

Another new theme clearly derives from the pounding rhythmic figure from the slow introduction **[T5/i3, 3:02],** answered as before by a more lyrical figure in strings and woodwinds. The key is A-flat, the relative major of F minor and, therefore, a contrasting key by classical usage. This being Beethoven, however, the theme undergoes a momentary, striking harmonic change to the distant key of A at (3:14) but returns to a proper cadence in A-flat at (3:37).

The development **[T5/i4, 3:41]** is quite short and, within this context, rather cheery; it consists of a stepwise sequence: a questioning phrase derived from the "A" section of the principal theme, answered by the full orchestra, then the same process repeated, moving up the scale. The mood darkens, however, **[T5/i4, 4:10]** as the lower strings begin to rumble with reminiscences of "A" in its original, grumpy mood and whispers of the rhythmic shape of "B," leading inexorably to a recapitulation **[T5/i5, 4:28]** of the first and second themes much as before, except that the second theme—previously encountered in A-flat—now returns **[T5/i6, 5:35]** in D-flat, "balancing" the order of keys according to sonata-form principles. The horns now pick up the rhythmic figure **[T5/i6, 6:12]** and inaugurate a big buildup toward some kind of climax.

They ram the tonal center back to F minor (where it all had begun). Then: silence, and the audience hangs in suspense.

"March on, brave nation! The Goddess of Victory leads you!" Egmont achieves the triumphant martyrdom to the tune of this "Symphony of Victory" **[T5/i7, 6:52],** ushered in over an insistent roll on the timpani, with the shrill insistence of the piccolo (hitherto unused in the *Overture*) adding to the glory. A new theme in quarter notes **[T5/i7, 7:18]** is passed around from one part of the orchestra to another, leading to a huge, fanfarelike conclusion (7:47). (Compare this brassy conquest, piccolo and all, to the endings of Beethoven's *Fifth* and *Ninth Symphonies*. It compares very well.)

Basic Beethoven:
The Essential Recordings

1 **Symphony No. 3 in E-flat (Eroica), Op. 55; Overture to "Egmont," Op. 84.** Sir Georg Solti conducting the Chicago Symphony Orchestra. London 430 087-2.

See the Play-by-Play chapter for a detailed journey through these works.

2 **Symphony No. 9 in D minor, Opus 125.** Kurt Masur conducting the Leipzig Gewandhaus Orchestra and Radio Chorus, with Sylvia McNair, soprano; Jard van Nes, contralto; Uwe Heilmann, tenor; and Bernd Weikl, baritone. Philips 432 995-2.

There is a sense of inevitability in this work; when the chorus bursts forth with their "Hymn to Joy" to the words of Schiller, it could very well be the only kind of music to follow the sublime spirituality of the adagio. Certainly the wordless argument that rages at the start of the finale (itself a stupendous invention) presents no alternative. Even though the finale is the work's most startling forward step, the first movement is equally amazing: a deep, troubled, fierce struggle that proceeds from the distant cloudscape at the start to the bottomless pit of nameless tragedy nearly twenty minutes later.

Track 1:

First movement: Allegro ma non troppo, un poco maestoso

0:00 Introduction: subject in dominant key: violins

0:27 Principal theme, part I, in tonic key: full orchestra (tutti)

0:40 Principal theme, part II: tutti

1:04 Subject: D minor

1:27 Principal theme, part I: B flat major

1:48 Bridge passage to subordinate theme

2:06 Subordinate theme, part I, B flat major: winds

2:16 Subordinate theme, part II: winds/strings

2:30 Subordinate theme, part III: flute

2:37 Subordinate theme, part IV: strings

2:54 First intermediate motive: tutti

3:09 Second intermediate motive: violins

3:26 Third intermediate motive: strings

3:47 Fourth intermediate motive: tutti

3:57 Concluding theme (codetta), part I

4:11 Concluding theme (codetta), part II

4:41 Development section (subject)

6:12 Fugal development

7:17 Further development

8:25 Returning passage (transition)

8:46 Return of principal theme, parts I, II: D minor

9:27 Return of subordinate theme, parts I-IV: winds/strings: D major

10:16 Return of first intermediate motive

10:31 Return of second intermediate motive: E flat major

10:48 Return of third and fourth intermediate motives

11:22 Return of concluding theme (codetta), parts I, II

11:56 Coda begins

13:05 Coda continues: D major horn; D minor strings

14:03 Coda continues: winds

14:21 Coda continues: new material

15:15 Conclusion of coda

Track 2:

Second movement: Molto vivace (scherzo)

0:00 Part I: introductory motive: D minor

0:05 Principal theme (fughetta)

0:29 Principal theme (regular form)

0:39 Subordinate theme, part I: C major

0:47 Subordinate theme, part II

1:00 Concluding theme, modulating back to D minor

1:18 Repeat of principal theme through concluding theme

2:30 Part II: bridge passages

2:46 Principal theme: new form: winds

2:55 Principal theme developed: introductory motive: timpani

3:22 Returning transitional passage

3:33 Return of principal theme

3:46 Return of subordinate theme, parts I and II

4:17 Return of concluding theme (codetta)

4:28 Bridge passage

4:41 Returning transitional passage

4:52 Trio section: principal theme: winds: D major

5:04 First interlude: strings

5:18 Principal theme: horns and strings

5:28 Second interlude: oboes and bassoons

5:51 Principal theme: winds and strings

6:05 Repeat of preceding trio material (from 5:04 to 6:04)

7:05 Coda: final statements of principal theme

7:40 Return to minor mode

7:45 Scherzo da capo: introductory motive: part I: D minor

7:50 Principal theme (fughetta)

8:14 Principal theme (regular form)

8:24 Subordinate theme: parts I and II: C major

8:44 Concluding theme: modulating back to D minor

9:01 Part II: bridge passages

9:17 Principal theme: new form: winds

9:26 Principal theme developed: introductory motive: timpani

9:52 Returning transitional passage

10:04 Return of principal theme

10:16 Return of subordinate theme, parts I and II

10:46 Return of concluding theme (codetta)

10:58 Bridge passage

11:12 Coda

Track 3:

Third Movement: Adagio molto e cantabile

0:00 Introduction

0:14 Exposition: principal theme, part I: strings: B flat major

1:11 Principal theme, part II

2:21 Andante moderato: subordinate theme: strings: D major

3:38 Tempo primo: first variation of principal theme: violins: B flat major

4:34 First variation of principal theme, part II

5:48 Andante: return of subordinate theme: flute and winds: G major

7:00 Adagio: second variation of principal theme: clarinet, horn, bassoon: E flat major

8:21 Lo stesso tempo: third variation of principal theme, part I: violins: B flat major

9:16 Second variation of principal theme, part II: oboe and violins

10:26 Intermediate motive (tutti)

10:57 Fourth variation of principal theme, part I 11:35 Return of intermediate motive: tutti

11:51 Modulatory bridge passage: D flat major, E flat minor, B flat minor

12:20 Final variation of principal theme: B flat major

13:55 Coda

Tracks 4-10:

Fourth movement

Track 4:

Presto

0:00 Tutti introduction: principal motive (D minor, forte)

0:10 Quasi-recitative passage: cellos and basses preview baritone singer

0:25 Return of principal motive

0:33 Quasi-recitative passage

0:44 Motto signal from first movement

0:57 Quasi-recitative passage

1:18 Theme from second movement scherzo

1:25 Quasi-recitative passage

1:42 Theme from third movement adagio

1:51 Quasi-recitative passage

2:12 Suggestion of folk song motive

2:17 Quasi-recitative passage

2:38 Principal theme (folk song): cellos and basses

3:25 Principal theme: add bassoon and violas

4:08 Principal theme: add violins

4:51 Principal theme: tutti

5:29 Concluding theme (codetta)

5:54 Returning passage: transition

Track 5:

Presto (continued)

0:00 Return of introduction motive

0:08 Baritone recitative: "O Freunde..."

Track 6:

Ode "To Joy": allegro assai

0:00 Antiphonal introduction: baritone, chorus

0:07 Baritone solo: stanza 1: D major

0:36 Chorus: stanza 1, second half

0:50 Bridge passage

0:56 Solo quartet: stanza 2, variation I

1:24 Chorus: stanza 2, second half

1:38 Bridge passage

1:44 Solo quartet: stanza 3, variation II

2:12 Chorus: stanza 3, second half

2:25 Bridge passage with chorus: modulation to B flat major

3 *Symphonies No. 5 in C minor, Op. 67* and *No. 7 in A, Op. 92.*
Bernard Haitink conducting the Royal Concertgebouw Orchestra of Amsterdam. Philips 420 540-2.

It's hard to envision the effects these works must have had on their first audiences: the *Fifth*, with its unifying, obsessive melodic gambit; the *Seventh*, with its breathless, whirling dance rhythms. Actually, the *Fifth* is more closely akin to the *Eroica* than most people realize, the progression from a chaotic madness at the start to the triumphant finale. The *Seventh* is, above all, the pronouncement of a composer absolutely confident of his omnipotence. He was, of course, right.

TRACKS 1-4:

Symphony No. 5 in C minor, Op. 67

Track 1:
Allegro con brio Sonata form

0:00 Exposition: first theme
0:47 Second theme
1:06 Third theme
1:24 Exposition (repeat): first theme
2:10 Second theme
2:29 Third theme
2:48 Development: first theme
3:23 Second theme
4:11 Recapitulation: first theme
4:58 Second theme
5:28 Third theme
5:41 Coda (based on first theme)

Track 2:
Andante con moto
Theme and variations

0:00 Theme
1:17 First variation
2:03 Second variation
3:16 Third variation (based on first variation)
4:01 Fourth variation
5:13 Fifth variation
5:58 Sixth variation (based on first variation)

6:44 Seventh variation

7:25 Eighth variation

8:14 Ninth variation

9:09 Tenth variation (coda)

Track 3:

Allegro
Ternary form ABA

0:00 Part A: first theme

0:22 Second theme

1:17 Both first and second themes

1:48 Part B: first theme

2:45 First theme (return)

3:15 Part A: first theme (variation)

3:35 Second theme (variation)

3:55 Both first and second themes
(variation)

4:27 Coda

Track 4:

Allegro
Sonata form

0:00 Exposition: first theme

0:37 Second theme

1:06 Third theme

1:34 Fourth theme

2:13 First development: third theme

3:43 Second theme (from movement
III, track 3)

4:18 Recapitulation: first theme

4:54 Second theme

5:26 Third theme

5:54 Fourth theme

6:26 Second development/coda:
third theme

6:58 Second theme

7:55 Fourth theme

8:13 First theme

TRACKS 5-8:

Symphony No. 7 in A, Op. 92

Track 5:

Poco sostenuto: vivace
Sonata form

0:00 Introduction: first theme

0:57 First theme (development)

1:27 Second theme

2:09 First theme (return)

2:38 Second theme (return and
development)

3:19 Transition to exposition

4:02 Exposition: first theme

4:54 Second them

5:36 Third theme

6:20 Exposition (repeat): first theme

7:17 Second theme

7:59 Third theme

8:47 Development: first theme

10:43 Recapitulation: first theme

11:43 Second theme

12:21 Third theme

13:06 Coda (based on first theme)

Track 6:
Allegretto
Theme and variations

0:00 Introduction to theme

0:51 First theme

1:38 First variation

2:25 Second variation

3:17 Second theme

4:50 Third variation

5:52 Fourth variation (fugue)

6:50 First coda (based on fourth variation)

7:11 Second theme (partial)

8:11 Second coda

Track 7:
Presto: Assai meno presto

0:00 First theme

0:23 First theme (development)

2:26 Second theme

2:58 First theme (partial return)

3:24 First theme (return)

3:43 Second theme (return)

4:51 First theme (return)

6:15 Second theme (return)

7:57 First theme (return)

9:11 Coda

Track 8:
Allegro con brio
Sonata form

0:00 Exposition: first theme

0:43 Second theme

0:56 Third theme

1:40 Fourth theme

1:58 Development: second theme

2:15 First theme

3:12 First theme (variation)

3:34 Recapitulation: first theme

4:00 Second theme

4:13 Third theme

5:00 Fourth theme

5:20 Coda (first and second themes)

4 *Piano Concertos No. 4 in G, Op. 58* and *No. 5 in E-flat, Op. 73 (The Emperor)*. Vladimir Ashkenazy, pianist, with Zubin Mehta conducting the Vienna Philharmonic Orchestra. London 430 704-2.

Both concertos bring on the soloist in the first measures, as a teaser for what will eventually come from the piano. But listen to what happens at the start of the supremely lyrical, richly humanistic *Fourth*: no sooner has the pianist offered up the first phrase of the principal theme than the orchestra responds in a jolting, distant key. The same thing happens at the end of the mysterious, cloudy slow movement of the *Emperor*, where suddenly piano and orchestra softly slide from one tonality to another, distant one. Beethoven wrote his concertos for himself, but he was too far into his own silent world to manage the imperial majesty of the *Emperor*.

TRACKS 1-3:

Concerto No. 4 in G, Op. 58

Track 1:
Allegro moderato Sonata form

0:00 First exposition: first theme: piano

0:21 First theme: orchestra

1:23 Second theme

2:13 Third theme (based on second theme)

2:41 Fourth theme

2:58 Second exposition: with piano, first theme

3:14 First theme (variation)

4:25 Second theme (variation)

5:01 Third theme (variation)

5:37 Second theme (return)

6:31 Third theme (return)

7:34 Fourth theme (return)

7:52 Development: first theme

10:49 First recapitulation: first theme of first exposition: piano

11:04 First theme: orchestra

11:49 Second theme

12:21 Third theme: with piano

12:58 Second theme (return)

13:51 Third theme (return)

14:28 Third theme: with piano

14:57 Cadenza: first theme: piano

15:35 Third theme

17:27 Third theme (interrupted by first theme)

18:46 Second recapitulation: third theme

19:21 First theme (used as closing material)

Track 2:

Andante con moto

0:00 First theme: orchestra

0:19 First theme: piano

1:46 Second theme: piano

3:01 Third theme: piano

3:35 Cadenza-like section

4:41 First theme: orchestra (re-entrance)

Track 3:

Rondo

0:00 First theme

1:12 Second theme

1:40 Third theme, part I

2:01 Third theme, part II

2:32 First theme

4:36 Second theme

5:05 Third theme, part I

5:25 Third theme, part II

5:38 Development (all themes)

6:40 First theme (variation)

7:10 Second theme (variation)

7:51 Cadenza (based on first theme)

8:08 Cadenza (continued, based on second theme)

8:43 Orchestral re-entrance

9:39 First theme (final entrance)

TRACKS 4–6:

Concerto No. 5 in E flat, Op. 73

Track 4:

Allegro, Sonata form

0:00 Introduction

1:15 First exposition: first theme

2:30 Second theme

2:55 First theme (return)

3:25 Third theme (based on first theme)

4:29 Second exposition: first theme: with piano

6:21 Second theme

7:45 Third theme

8:19 Development: first theme

8:47 Third theme

9:54 First theme (variation)

12:41 Recapitulation: introduction

13:23 First theme (return)

15:06 Second theme

15:41 First theme (return)

17:04 Coda: first theme

17:40 Cadenza (based on first theme)

18:07 Cadenza (continued, based on second theme)

18:24 Orchestral re-entrance

Track 5:

Adagio un poco mosso

0:00 First theme

1:56 Second theme

2:40 First theme (interrupts)

2:53 Second theme (continues)

3:14 First and second themes in combination

4:29 Third theme

5:46 Third theme (variation)

7:46 Coda

Track 6:

Allegro
Sonata form

0:00 Exposition: first theme, part I: piano

0:24 First theme, part I: orchestra

0:54 First theme, part II

1:13 Second theme

1:49 Third theme

2:23 Exposition (repeat): first theme: piano

2:49 First theme: orchestra

3:30 Development (variations): first variation

4:06 Second variation

4:46 Third variation

6:13 Recapitulation: first theme, part I: piano

6:33 First theme, part I: orchestra

7:03 First theme, part II

7:20 Second theme

8:00 Third theme

8:33 Coda: first theme, part I

9:57 First theme, part II

10:38 Brief cadenza

10:45 Final statement of first theme

5 ***Trio in D, Op. 70, No. 1 (The Ghost)*** and ***Trio in B-flat, Op. 97 (The Archduke)*.** The Beaux Arts Trio: Menaham Pressler, piano; Isidore Cohen, violin; and Bernard Greenhouse, cello. Philips 412 891-2.

The piano trio became the most popular chamber-music medium around 1800. The proper Viennese home boasted a piano, a daughter to play it, and a couple of string players to sit in; in the days before stereo, one could buy trio arrangements of practically everything to play at home: symphonies, even operas. These two works of Beethoven's aren't arrangements of anything, however, except that some of the music in the slow movement of the *Ghost* trio had originally been created for the Witches' Scene in the never-realized opera of *Macbeth*; hence, the title. *The Archduke* was based on a more corporeal figure, the benevolent Archduke Rudolph, a fair pianist, who is honored here in this most expansive, grandest, and most affectionate of all piano trios.

TRACKS 1-3:

Trio No. 4 in D, Op. 70, No. 1

Track 1:

Allegro vivace e con brio
Sonata form

0:00 Exposition: first theme
0:10 Second theme
0:40 Third theme
1:27 First theme (return)
1:34 Second theme (return)
2:04 Third theme (return)
2:51 Development: first theme
3:02 Second theme
3:51 First theme (return)
4:27 Recapitulation: first theme
4:45 Second theme
5:16 Third theme

6:20 Development (repeat): first theme

6:31 Second theme

7:19 First theme (second repeat)

7:56 Recapitulation (repeat): first theme

8:03 Second theme

8:46 Third theme

9:47 Coda

Track 2:

Largo assai ed espressivo
Sonata form

0:00 First Exposition: first theme

1:06 Second theme

1:46 Third theme

2:13 First development: first theme4:40 Second theme

5:00 First theme (return)

5:31 Second exposition: first theme

6:32 Second theme

7:09 Third theme

7:35 Second development: first theme

9:57 Second theme

10:27 First theme (return)

10:40 Coda (using material of third theme)

Track 3:

Presto
Sonata form

0:00 Exposition: first theme

0:44 Second theme

1:39 Third theme

2:08 Exposition (repeat): first theme

2:51 Second theme

3:45 Third theme

4:16 Development: third theme

4:36 First theme

5:14 Recapitulation: first theme

6:01 Second theme

6:56 Third theme

7:37 Coda

TRACKS 4-7:

Trio No. 6 in B flat, Op. 97

Track 4:
Allegro moderato
Sonata form

0:00 Exposition: first theme

0:36 First theme: with violin

1:20 First theme (variation)

2:00 Second theme

3:13 Third theme

3:42 Exposition (repeat): first theme

5:00 First theme (variation)

5:41 Second theme

6:53 Third theme

7:24 Development: third theme

7:40 First theme

10:15 Recapitulation: first theme

11:45 Second theme

12:56 Third theme

13:25 Coda

Track 5:

Scherzo
Ternary form ABA

0:00 Part A: first theme

0:28 First variation

0:54 Second variation

1:15 Third variation

1:35 Fourth variation

1:53 Part B: second theme (fugal exposition)

2:26 Third theme

2:58 Third theme (return)

3:16 Second theme (development)

3:50 Third theme (return)

4:14 Part A: first theme

4:40 First variation

5:06 Second variation

5:26 Third variation

5:46 Fourth variation

6:03 Coda

Track 6:

Andante cantabile ma però con moto

0:00 First part: first theme: with piano

0:37 First theme: with strings

1:22 First theme: with piano

1:58 Closing material: tutti

2:23 Second part

4:06 Third part

5:14 Fourth part

6:37 Fifth part: theme in piano, right hand

7:28 Fifth part: theme in strings

8:18 Fifth part (repeat): theme in piano, right hand

9:03 Fifth part (repeat): theme in strings

10:42 Closing material

11:50 Closing material (variation)

Track 7:

Allegro moderato
Rondo and variations

- **0:00** First theme
- **0:59** Second theme
- **1:24** First theme (return)
- **2:06** Third theme
- **2:55** First theme (variation)
- **3:58** Second theme (return)
- **4:58** First theme (variation)

6 ***Violin Sonatas No. 5 in F, Op. 24 (Spring)*** and in ***A, Op. 47 (Kreutzer).*** Itzhak Perlman, violin; Vladimir Ashkenazy, piano. London 410 554-2.

Beethoven's early works for violin and piano tended to favor the keyboard over the stringed instrument (as did those of Mozart); the *Spring*, with its ravishing melodic outpouring and frolicsome scherzo, was the first in which the two roles were equalized. (Nobody knows who gave the work its name; publishers did that sort of thing back then to sell more copies.) The *A-major Sonata*, on the other hand, takes its name from the French violinist Rodolphe Kreutzer, for whom it was intended (but who never played it). This was the first truly dramatic violin sonata, striding all over the place from major to minor, allotting some of its most important ideas to the violin unaccompanied, and working up a fine froth in the last movement, something close to the Italian tarantella.

TRACKS 1-3:

Sonata No. 9 in A, Op. 47

Track 1:

Adagio sostenuto/Presto/Adagio Sonata form

0:00	Introduction: first theme: with violin
0:30	First theme: with piano
1:23	Second theme
1:55	Exposition: first theme
3:07	Second theme
3:42	First theme (variation)
4:05	Third theme (based on first theme)
4:57	Development: third theme
7:15	Second theme (of introduction)
7:24	Recapitulation: first theme
8:23	Second theme
8:58	First theme (variation)

9:23 Third theme

10:08 Coda: first theme

10:23 First theme (development)

11:25 First theme (finale)

Andante con variazioni
Theme and variations

0:00 First theme: with piano

0:22 First theme: with violin

2:39 First variation

4:53 Second variation

6:46 Third variation

9:46 Fourth variation

13:03 Introduction to fifth variation

13:30 Fifth variation

15:46 Coda

Presto
Sonata form

0:00 Exposition: first theme, part I

0:43 First theme, part II

1:08 First theme, part III

1:27 Second theme

1:48 Third theme (based on first theme)

2:05 Exposition (repeat): first

theme, part I

2:45 First theme, part II

3:10 First theme, part III

3:29 Second theme

3:51 Third theme

4:08 Development: first theme (complete)

5:28 Recapitulation: first theme, part I (minor)

5:59 First theme, part II

6:24 First theme, part III

6:42 Second theme

7:06 Third theme

7:23 Coda

7:49 Adagio (variation of first theme)

8:21 Final development of first theme

TRACKS 4-7:

Sonata No. 5 in F, Op. 24

Track 4:
Allegro
Sonata form

0:00 Exposition: first thematic group

1:10 Second thematic group

2:01 Third theme

2:29 Exposition (repeat): first group

3:39 Second group

4:31 Third theme

4:58 Development: first group

5:06 Second group

6:01 Recapitulation: first thematic group

7:14 Second group

8:06 Third theme

8:33 Coda

Track 5:
Adagio molto espressivo

0:05 First theme: in piano

0:45 First theme: in violin

1:25 Second theme

2:27 First theme (variation): piano

3:09 First theme (variation): violin

4:27 Second theme (development): piano

4:49 Second theme (development): violin

5:55 First theme (development)

Track 6:
Scherzo and trio

0:00 Scherzo

0:25 Trio

0:46 Scherzo (repeat)

Track 7:
Finale

0:00 First theme

0:28 Second theme

1:01 Third theme

1:30 First theme (first variation)

1:56 Second theme (first variation)

2:50 Coda

3:03 First theme (second variation)

3:51 Second theme (return)

4:24 Third theme (return)

5:08 First theme (third variation)

5:35 Second theme (second variation)

6:31 Second theme (drive to close)

7 ***String Quartet in B-flat, Op. 130*** with the ***Grosse Fuge in B-flat, Op. 133.*** Guarneri Quartet. Philips 422 059-2.

In the depths of depression, brought on by matters concerning nephew Karl and the deafness that led to embarrassment at a *Fidelio* rehearsal, Beethoven received a life-restoring commission from Count Galitzin that resulted in this group of profound, quasi-mystical string quartets that are the unquestioned masterpieces of the idiom. The *B-flat Quartet* is a work of many moods: a lighthearted, joking slow movement; another slow movement (titled "cavatina") that stops the breath with its sublime melodic flow; a quiet, amiable dance marked "Alla tedesca"; and, at the end, a furious, intricate, grinding fugue, half again as long as the rest of the quartet. Friends and publishers later convinced Beethoven to substitute a gentler last movement, for fear of exhausting both the musicians and the audience. He substituted a charming, shorter movement (it was the last completed music from his pen) and published the original finale separately as the *Grosse Fuge* ("Great Fugue"). It is, indeed, a killer, thriller of a piece. One can, of course, program the compact disc to skip Track 6 and move on to Track 7, thus re-creating the sweat and shock of the work's first performance.

TRACKS 1-6:

Quartet No. 13 in B flat, Op. 130

Track 1:

Adagio ma non troppo/Allegro
Sonata form

0:00 Exposition: introduction, part I

0:37 Introduction: part II

1:13 First theme, part I

1:45 First theme, part I (return)

2:06 First theme, part II

2:37 Second theme

3:15 Second theme: development

3:52 Third theme

4:04 Exposition: repeat

8:03 Development: based on introduction

8:35 First theme

9:40 Recapitulation: first theme, part I

10:04 First theme, part II (variation)

10:33 Second theme (variation)

11:04 Second theme (return)

12:16 Third theme (return)

12:30 Coda

Track 2:

Presto
ABA form

0:00 A

0:25 B

1:13 Transition

1:20 A (return)

Track 3:

Andante con moto ma non troppo
Binary form

0:00 A: introduction

0:13 First theme

0:47 Transition

1:04 Second theme

1:34 First theme (variation)

1:53 Third theme

2:53 B: introduction

3:04 First theme

3:37 Transition

3:54 Second theme

4:25 First theme (variation)

4:44 Third theme

5:24 Coda

6:21 Third theme

6:35 Third theme: development

5:20 Part II: third theme (return)

6:00 Third theme (several fugue-like entrances)

6:40 Third theme (fragments)

7:04 Third theme (variation)

8:01 Part III: second theme (return)

8:33 Second theme: fugue

9:40 Second theme: fugue (abridged)

10:34 Second theme (variation)

11:08 Second theme (further variation)

11:45 Part IV: third theme (return)

12:22 Transition

12:49 Part V: second theme (return)

13:16 Second theme (development)

13:59 First theme (return)

14:40 Part VI: fugue (based on part I)

14:53 First theme (return)

15:41 Part I (variation)

8 **Piano Sonatas No. 8 in C minor, Op. 13 (Pathétique); No. 14 in C-sharp minor, Op. 27, No. 2 (Moonlight); No. 23 in F minor, Op. 57 (Appassionata).** Alfred Brendel, pianist. Philips 411 470-2.

A sense of what it must have been like to hear Beethoven at the piano comes across in these well-known sonatas: the fury, the onslaught of dense pileups of notes and chords that express Beethoven's impatience with the instruments of his time, the wonderful soft piano tone in such movements as the opening of the *Moonlight* or the slow variations in the *Appassionata*. (None of these sonatas, by the way, were named by Beethoven; they all represent the hopes of their publisher to sweeten the market with fancy verbiage.) These works make it clear that Beethoven trusted the piano as well as the orchestra to carry forth his tense, personal dramatic visions.

TRACKS 1-3:

Sonata No. 14 in C-sharp minor, Op. 27, No. 2

Track 1:
Adagio sostenuto
Quasi sonata form

0:00 Introduction
0:26 First theme
1:17 Second theme
1:58 Development: first theme

3:33 Recapitulation: first theme
4:21 Second theme
5:05 Coda

Track 2:
Allegretto
Ternary form ABA

0:00 Part A: theme
1:00 Part B: theme
1:45 Part A: theme (return)

Track 3:

Presto agitato
Sonata form

0:00 Exposition: first theme

0:32 Second theme

1:05 Third theme

1:28 Fourth theme

1:41 Exposition (repeat): first theme

2:13 Second theme

2:47 Third theme

3:09 Fourth theme

3:23 Development: first theme

3:33 Second theme

4:26 Recapitulation: first theme

4:49 Second theme

5:23 Third theme

5:46 Fourth theme

5:59 Coda

6:34 Cadenza

TRACKS 4-6:

Sonata No. 8 in C minor, Op. 13

Track 4:

Grave and allegro di molto e con brio
Sonata form

0:00 Introduction

2:14 First theme

2:45 Second theme

3:15 Third theme

3:55 Exposition (repeat): first theme

4:22 Second theme

4:53 Third theme

5:30 Development: introduction

6:24 First theme

7:09 Recapitulation: first theme

7:29 Second theme

7:55 Third theme

8:37 Coda

Track 5:

Adagio cantabile

0:00 First theme

1:13 Second theme

2:10 First theme (return)

2:47 Third theme

3:31 First theme (variation)

4:28 Coda

Track 6:
Rondo allegro
Rondo form

0:00 First theme

0:20 Second theme

1:15 First theme (return)

1:34 Third theme

2:29 First theme (variation)

2:55 Second theme (variation)

3:34 First theme (abridged)

3:45 Second theme (variation)

4:16 First theme (final return)

TRACKS 7-9:

Sonata No. 23 in F minor, Op. 57

Track 7:
Assai allegro
Sonata form

0:00 Exposition: first theme

0:59 Second theme

1:21 First theme (variation)

1:58 Third theme

2:27 Development: first theme

3:30 Second theme

4:52 Third theme

4:57 Recapitulation: first theme

5:59 Second theme

6:59 Third theme

7:30 Coda

Track 8:
Andante con moto
Theme and variations

0:00 First theme

1:43 First variation

3:06 Second variation

4:19 Third variation

5:30 Fourth variation

Track 9:
Allegro ma non troppo
Sonata form

0:00 Exposition: introduction

0:16 First theme

1:04 Second theme

1:22 Third theme (based on first theme)

1:40 Development: first theme

3:06 Recapitulation: first theme

3:54 Second theme

4:10 Third theme

4:28 Development (repeat): first theme

5:55 Recapitulation (repeat): first theme

6:43 Second theme

6:59 Third theme

7:15 Coda

9 *Missa Solemnis in D, Opus 123; Mass in C, Opus 86.* Colin Davis conducting the London Symphony Orchestra and Chorus, with Anna Tomowa-Sintow, soprano; Patricia Payne, mezzo-soprano; Robert Tear, tenor; and Robert Lloyd, bass. Philips 2-438363-2 (two discs).

Beethoven composed two extended settings of the text of the Catholic Mass, the quiet, reverent C-major work from about the time of the "Emperor" *Concerto* and the huge, overpowering *Solemn Mass* near the end of his life. He wrote the latter as a tribute to his friend and patron the Archduke Rudolph on his elevation to a high religious post; the work was not, however, completed in time for the ceremony. Even in its finished form, the music is full of struggle: the counterpoint in the choral writing, the cruel high notes for the vocal soloists...it is the one great work of Beethoven's that clearly displays the cruelty of his physical condition as he grappled with it. The result, for all its flaws, is one of the world's most majestic choral masterpieces.

DISC 1

Missa Solemnis, beginning

Track 1:

Kyrie
Assai sostenuto

- **0:00** Part I: first theme: orchestra: D major
- **0:22** Second theme: orchestra (solo clarinet): G major
- **0:31** Third theme: orchestra
- **1:04** First theme: chorus: "Kyrie"
- **1:07** Second theme: tenor solo: "Kyrie"
- **1:35** Third theme: alto solo/chorus: "Kyrie eleison"
- **2:59** Fourth theme (variation of third theme): chorus (in canon): "Eleison"
- **4:18** Part II: andante assai ben marcato: solo quartet: "Christe": B minor
- **5:03** First theme: chorus: "Christe"
- **5:27** First theme (variation): chorus/solo quartet: "Christe"
- **6:06** Part I (return): first theme: orchestra
- **6:42** First theme (return): chorus/solo quartet: "Kyrie"
- **9:34** Fifth theme: chorus: "Eleison"
- **10:38** First theme (final variation): chorus

TRACKS 2-4:

Gloria

Track 2:

Gloria
Allegro vivace

- **0:00** Part I: orchestra: first theme: D major
- **0:05** First theme: chorus: "Gloria"
- **0:21** Second theme: chorus: "in excelsis"
- **0:33** First theme: chorus: "Gloria"
- **0:49** Third theme: bass chorus: "Et in terra"
- **1:20** First theme (variation): chorus: "Laudamus te"
- **1.41** Fourth theme: chorus: "Glorificamus": D major
- **2:06** Fourth theme (variation): chorus: "Glorificamus": G major
- **2:40** Part II: meno allegro: first theme: orchestra/chorus: "Gratias"

3:29 First theme (variation): chorus: "Gratias"

3:48 First theme (variation of first theme, part I): "Domine" E flat major

4:13 Second theme: solo quartet: "Domine fili"

4:32 Third theme: chorus: "Domine deus" F major

Track 3:

Qui tollis
Larghetto

0:00 Development: orchestra

0:34 First theme: solo quartet: "Qui tollis": F major

1:08 First theme (answer): chorus: "Miserere"

1:51 First theme (variation): chorus: "Qui tollis": D major

3:03 Second theme: chorus/solo quartet: "Qui sedes": B flat major

3:30 Third theme: solo quartet: "Miserere"

Track 4:

Quoniam
Allegro maestoso

0:00 Part I: first theme: orchestra

0:11 First theme: chorus: "Quoniam": D major

1:03 Second theme: chorus: "Cum sancto"

1:36 Part II: allegro ma non troppo: fugue: first theme: chorus: "In gloria"

4:03 First theme (variation): solo quartet/chorus: "In gloria"

4:28 First theme (variation, condensed fugue): chorus: "In gloria"

5:07 Part III: poco più allegro: solo quartet: "Amen": D major

6:40 Part IV: presto (return of first theme from Gloria, track 2): "Gloria"

TRACKS 5-7:

Credo

Credo
Allegro ma non troppo

- **0:00** First theme: orchestra/chorus: "Credo": B flat major
- **1:25** First theme (return): chorus: "Credo"
- **2:32** Second theme: chorus: "Deum de deum": G major
- **2:53** Third theme: chorus: "Consubstantialem"
- **3:39** Fourth theme: chorus: "Qui propter nos homines"
- **3:58** Fifth theme: chorus: "Descendit"

Et incarnatus est
Adagio

- **0:00** First theme, part I: chorus/solo quartet: "Et incarnatus"
- **1:27** First theme, part II: chorus
- **1:37** Second theme (development): andante: chorus/tenor solo: "Et homo"
- **2:23** Third theme: adagio espressivo: solo quartet: "Crucifixus"

- **3:32** Fourth theme: quartet/chorus: "Passus": sequence of keys
- **6:04** Fifth theme (development): allegro: chorus: "Et resurrexit"
- **6:20** Sixth theme: chorus: "Et ascendit": C major
- **6:50** Seventh theme: chorus: "Judicare": sequence of keys
- **7:13** First theme (variation): chorus: "Cuius regni"

Credo
Allegro ma non troppo

- **0:00** Part I: first theme (variation of first theme, track 5): chorus: "Credo"
- **1:38** Part II: allegretto ma non troppo: first theme: chorus: "Et vitam"
- **4:37** Part III: allegro con moto: first theme (variation of part II): "Et vitam"
- **6:30** Part IV: grave: first theme: chorus/solo quartet: "Et vitam": B flat major

TRACKS 8-9:

Sanctus/Benedictus

Track 8:

Sanctus
Adagio

0:00 Part I: first theme: orchestra: D major

1:01 First theme: solo quartet: "Sanctus"

1:48 First theme (return): solo quartet: "Sanctus"

3:07 Part II: allegro pesante: chorus: "Pleni sunt": D major

3:53 Part III: presto: first theme: chorus: "Osanna"

Track 9:

Preludium/Benedictus
Sostenuto

0:00 Introduction: orchestra

2:04 Solo violin entrance

2:26 First theme: chorus bass/solo violin: "Benedictus"

4:00 Second theme: solo alto/bass: "Benedictus": G major

4:40 Second theme: solo soprano/tenor: "Benedictus"

5:42 Third theme: chorus: "In nomine"

7:31 Second theme (variation): solo quartet: "Benedictus"

9:14 Third theme (variation): chorus: "In nomine"

9:38 First theme (variation): solo quartet: "Qui venit"

10:43 Fourth theme: chorus: "Osanna": G major

DISC 2

TRACKS 1-3:

Missa Solemnis, conclusion

Track 1:

Agnus Dei
Adagio

0:00 First theme: orchestra/bass solo: "Agnus dei": B minor

1:13 Second theme: orchestra/chorus: "Miserere"

2:20 First theme (variation): alto/tenor solo: "Agnus"

3:15 Second theme (variation): alto solo/chorus: "Miserere"

4:23 First theme (variation): solo quartet: "Agnus"

5:19 Second theme (variation): chorus/solo quartet: "Miserere"

Track 2:

Dona nobis pacem
Allegretto vtvace

0:00 First theme: chorus: "Dona nobis": A major

0:34 Second theme: chorus: "Pacem": D major

1:07 Third theme: chorus: "Dona nobis"

1:45 Fourth theme (variation of third theme): chorus/soprano solo: "Dona"

Track 3:

Agnus dei
Allegro assai

0:00 Part I: development: orchestra

0:17 Development (quasi-recitative): solo quartet: "Agnus dei"

0:46 First theme (variation of first theme, track 2): quartet: "Dona nobis"

1:44 Second theme (variation of third theme, track 2): chorus: "Dona nobis"

3:02 Third theme (variation of fourth theme, track 2): chorus/solo quartet: "Dona nobis"

3:30 Part II: presto: orchestra: D Major

4:15 Development: chorus: "Agnus"

4:27 First theme: chorus/solo quartet: "Dona nobis": B flat major

4:38 Part III: first theme (variation of first theme, track 2): quartet: "Dona"

4:59 Second theme (variation): chorus: "Dona nobis": D major

5:19 Third theme: solo quartet: "Pacem"

5:41 Fourth theme: chorus: "Pacem" D Major

7:21 Fifth theme (variation of third theme, track 2): chorus: "Dona nobis"

TRACKS 4-12:

Mass in C, Op. 86

Track 4:

Kyrie
Andante con moto

0:00 First theme: chorus: "Kyrie": C Major

0:39 Second theme: soprano solo: "Kyrie"

0:56 Second theme: solo quartet/chorus: "Kyrie"

1:35 Third theme: solo quartet: "Christe": E major 2:58 First theme (variation):

chorus: "Kyrie": E major

4:07 Second theme (return): soprano solo: "Kyrie"

TRACKS 5-7:

Gloria

Track 5:

Gloria
Allegro con brio

0:00 First theme: chorus: "Gloria": C Major

0:29 Second theme: chorus: "Bonae voluntatis": A minor

1:45 Third theme: tenor solo/chorus: "Gratias agimus": B flat major

Track 6:

Qui tollis
Andante mosso

0:00 First theme: alto solo/chorus: "Qui tollis": F minor

0:41 First theme: solo quartet: "Qui tollis"

1:46 Second theme: chorus: "Qui sedes"

Track 7:

Quoniam
Allegro ma non troppo

0:00 First theme: orchestra: C major

0:14 First theme: chorus: "Quoniam"

0:34 Second theme: fugue: chorus: "Cum sancto": C major

2:53 Text painting: solo soprano/chorus: "Amen"

TRACKS 8-9:

Credo

Track 8:

Credo
Allegro con brio

0:00 First theme: chorus: "Credo": C major

0:24 Second theme: chorus: "Factorem": sequence of keys

0:42 First theme (variation): chorus: "Et in unum"

1:03 Third theme: chorus: "Ante omnia"

1:15 Fourth theme: chorus: "Deum de deo": E flat major

1:35 Fifth theme: chorus: "Consubstantialem": E flat major

2:06 Sixth theme: tenor/bass solo: "Qui propter nos homines"

Track 9:

Et incarnatus est
Adagio

0:00 Part I: first theme: solo quartet: "Et incarnatus": E flat major

1:13 Second theme: chorus: "Crucifixus": B flat minor and sequence of keys

1:58 Third theme: solo quartet: "Passus"

4:08 Part II: allegro ma non troppo: bass solo/chorus: "Et ascendit": D major

4:30 Second theme: chorus: "Sedet": C major

5:08 Third theme: chorus: "Cujus regni": G major

5:33 Fourth theme: solo quartet: "Et in spiritum"

6:05 Fifth theme: chorus: "Qui locutus est": C major

7:10 Part III: fugue: chorus: "Et vitam": C major

7:45 Fugue (variation): alto solo: "Et vitam": A major

Sanctus
Adagio

- **0:00** First theme: orchestra: A major
- **0:34** First theme: chorus: "Sanctus"
- **2:24** Second theme: allegro: chorus: "Pleni sunt coeli": D major
- **3:09** Third theme: chorus: "Osanna in excelsis"

Benedictus
Allegretto ma non troppo

- **0:00** First theme: solo quartet: "Benedictus": F major
- **0:32** Second theme: solo quartet: "Qui venit"
- **0:59** Third theme: quartet/chorus: "Benedictus": C major
- **2:26** Fourth theme: solo quartet: "Benedictus": F major
- **5:12** First theme (variation): solo quartet: "Benedictus": F major
- **6:40** Fifth theme (same as third theme, track 10): chorus: "Osanna"

Agnus Dei
Poco andante

- **0:00** First theme: chorus: "Agnus dei"
- **1:18** Second theme: chorus: "Miserere"
- **2:10** First theme (variation): chorus: "Agnus dei"
- **2:59** Second theme (variation): chorus: "Miserere"
- **3:33** Third theme: solo quartet: "Dona nobis"
- **4:38** Fourth theme: chorus: "Miserere"
- **5:34** Fifth theme: chorus: "Pacem"

Glossary

Arpeggio   The word comes from *arpa* (Italian for "harp"), and denotes a succession of at least three notes that outline a **harmony.** If played simultaneously, they would be a chord. Classical composers who wanted to define the **tonality** of a work at the outset often devised melodies that began by outlining the basic harmony of that tonality: for example, the first five notes of Beethoven's *First Piano Sonata.* Similarly, the *Eroica* begins with a tune that is really an E-flat arpeggio, but with the tenth note it goes wonderfully and dramatically wrong. The famous first *Prelude* in Bach's *Well-* *Tempered Clavier* is nothing but an arpeggiated sequence of harmonies.

Chamber music   A self-explanatory concept: music meant to be played in close surroundings, in a style that is intimate and subtle. Chamber music uses only a single instrument on a part, as opposed to orchestral music where several violins, violas, or cellos may be playing in unison. The sovereign chamber-music form, from the eighteenth century to the present, is the string quartet (two violins, viola, and cello). The piano trio (piano, violin, and cello) was also a popular chamber-music medium. With every instrument given equal importance, chamber music typifies democracy in action.

Chromatic In the most familiar harmonic system, the musical octave (from, say, C to C) is divided into twelve half-steps, also known as chromatic steps. The diatonic musical scale, which is the basis of a piece in a given **tonality**—C major, for example—is a pattern of seven tones from those possible twelve, an arrangement of half- and whole-steps. Any other notes—an F-sharp, say, in the key of C—are dissonances, the alien resources a composer uses to enrich his music, the friction that makes the wheels turn. Consider the tenth note in the *Eroica's* first melody: it's a dissonant note within Beethoven's chosen key. Listen to the way Beethoven "milks" that dissonance as that note seems to lean heavily into the next note which, being consonant (or nondissonant), is said to resolve the dissonance.

Classical At its purest, the term refers to the ancient world. The Classical revival in the eighteenth century used ancient models (such as the Parthenon) to define its passion for clear, logical structure in all the arts, and so the term is used to describe the works of this time. Used more loosely, "Classical" also refers to music that is meant to be heard against a background of silence by audiences trained to applaud only at its end—as opposed to "pop."

Concerto *Certare* means "to battle" or "to struggle"; *con* means "with." The concerto pits small forces against large: soloist and orchestra locked in wordless struggle. Mozart ennobled the form, turning his concertos into heartfelt "conversations" rather than mere showy pieces. Beethoven broadened the sense of drama; the slow movement of his *Fourth Piano Concerto* is a heartfelt "argument" between piano and orchestra.

Counterpoint or **polyphony** (the terms are synonymous) Many lines of music occurring simultaneously create a contrapuntal (or polyphonic) texture. In opera, the device allows for a stageful of characters, each expressing a different thought but all woven together. Haydn and Mozart discovered the music of

Bach, the supreme contrapuntal master, late in their own careers and were strongly impressed; the finale of Mozart's *Jupiter Symphony,* which interweaves five separate melodic lines, was one spectacular result. Beethoven's counterpoint is often violent, as in the *Grosse Fuge* for string quartet; he seems to be slamming the lines together and ordering them to adhere.

Enlightenment   The virtues of tolerance and brotherly love; the notion that men were born free and deserved to be free; a world view comprising a synthesis of God, man, and nature: these were the tenets of the intellectual movement upheld by Jean Jacques Rousseau, Voltaire (a pen name for François Marie Arouet), the proponents of the Classical revival, Johann Wolfgang von Goethe, and by such enlightened monarchs as Austria's Joseph II, who defied the excessive conservatism of Rome's church. "Enlightenment," wrote Immanuel Kant, "is a person's egress from the immaturity he had brought upon himself."

Form   In the broadest sense, musical form (or structure) is the composer's way of involving a listener's memory in the unfolding of a piece. One reacts to the initial music, follows a pathway to contrasting ideas, is stirred when the material returns or when the composer subjects it to new variations. The great composers are those who are most successful at finding ways to stretch the meaning of form to allow for individual expression. Some of the forms they worked with are fairly simple: the rondo, for example, intersperses constant reiteration of its main theme with other contrasting sections: A-B-A-C-A-D-A, etc. In variations, a single theme heard at the outset undergoes new complications at each return, while still clinging to its original outline.

Harmony   This refers to the ability to hear more than one tone at a time, to react to the way these simultaneous tones blend into a consonance or dissonance, and to follow the way one harmony will lead to the next to produce a progression. Dissonant harmonies set up an expectation; consonant harmonies resolve it into a feeling of arrival, and this process continues, again and again, sweeping the music to its stable, logical fulfillment.

Melody The horizontal aspect of music (as **harmony** is the vertical), the rising-falling line of expression that results from connecting the dots. Early music was nothing but melody, given a relationship to time (long notes versus short notes) by its rhythm. Other civilizations have built elaborate musical systems solely on melody; listen, for example, to the wonderful complexity of Indian classical music as played by Ravi Shankar—it is pure melody.

Movement This is a section of a longer work (concerto, symphony, sonata) which is musically complete in itself. In works of several movements, the composer usually arranges them to provide contrast: fast followed by slow, complex followed by simple. In Beethoven's time, audiences saw nothing wrong with separating the movements of a work with other composers' music in between and, therefore, applauded at the end of each movement.

Nineteenth-century composers began to see multimovement works as single expressions. Some audiences today still subscribe to the eighteenth-century practice, however.

Opera The emergence of opera is usually dated at the start of the seventeenth century, when several Italian composers sought to "reform" music by reviving the Greek ideal of sung drama. Two centuries later, Italy remained the prime proving ground, where singers reigned supreme and sensible plots were secondary. Yet the idea of reform persisted; in the 1760s, Christoph Willibald Gluck wrote music dramas that discouraged empty virtuosity in favor of serious plots abetted by serious music. With his *Abduction from the Seraglio* and *Magic Flute,* Mozart also raised the level of German opera from mere featherbrained burlesque to something more musically substantial. Beethoven's *Fidelio* continued this German tradition.

Sonata It simply means "sounded" or "played," as opposed to **cantata,** which means "sung." In Beethoven's time, the sonata was a piece for one instrument (keyboard) or two (violin and piano), in several movements. Symphonies, concertos, and string quartets are members of the sonata family as well, distinguished only by the performing forces they demand.

Sonata form It could just as easily be called "symphonic" form; it refers to the wonderfully logical and flexible organization of materials within an instrumental movement, practiced by composers in the Classical era and respected by composers of later times. The essence of the sonata form is contrast: between a first theme and melodies introduced later, between one tonality and another, between a slow rate of tonality change and a fast one, between the material when first heard and the subtle changes it undergoes later. With all those variables, sonata form became a great dramatic battlefield on which Beethoven could exercise with exquisite and awesome freedom. Only in the nineteenth century, by the way, was the whole notion of sonata form observed and codified by scholars. The great Classical composers never worked from rule books; they didn't need to.

Tonality (or **key**) From the Renaissance until early in the twentieth century, it was a given that Western music followed a system of tonality defined by the succession of harmonies derived from the notes of a given scale (see **chromatic**). The tonic of the key (the note C, for example, in the key of C) served as the point of origin, departure, and ultimate return; the music began in its given tonality, strayed somewhere else, and then returned, sometimes quite dramatically. The destiny of music, after the clear horizons of classicism, seems like an ongoing attempt to blur the sense of tonality: this is where the opening of the *Eroica* stands at a musical crossroads. The cloudy opening of Beethoven's *Ninth Symphony* is certainly a further step in that direction, much imitated by later composers. In the twentieth century, the innovative composer and theorist Arnold Schoenberg declared the integrity of nontonal (i.e., atonal) music, while also proclaiming that there was still plenty of good music waiting to be written in the key of C.

Further Reading and Listening

General Histories

Lang, Paul Henry. *Music in Western Civilization.* New York: W.W. Norton, 1941.

Pauly, Reinhard G. *Music in the Classic Period.* New Jersey: Prentice-Hall, 1965.

Rosen, Charles. *The Classical Style.* New York: W.W. Norton, 1972.

Schonberg, Harold. *Lives of the Great Composers.* New York: W.W. Norton, 1981.

Swafford, Jan. *The Vintage Guide to Classical Music.* New York: Vintage/Knopf, 1992.

Books on Beethoven

Cooper, Martin. *Beethoven, the Last Decade.* London: Oxford University Press, 1970.

Landon, H. C. Robbins. *Beethoven, Documentary Biography.* London: Macmillan, 1970.

Mellers, Wilfrid. *Beethoven and the Voice of God.* London: Faber and Faber, 1983.

Solomon, Maynard. *Beethoven.* New York: Schirmer, 1977.

Thayer, Alexander W. *Beethoven.* Revised and edited by Elliot Forbes. Princeton: Princeton University Press, 1967.

A Selective Beethoven Discography

Violin Concerto in D, Op. 61. Itzhak Perlman, with Carlo Maria Giulini and the Philharmonia Orchestra. EMI CDC 47002.

Choral Fantasy, Op. 80. Anthony Newman, on a period piano; Stephen Simon, conducting. Newport Classic 60031.

Fidelio, Op. 72. Jessye Norman, Reiner Goldberg, with Bernard Harlink conducting. Philips 426 308-2.

Quartets, Op. 18, Op. 59. Alban Berg Quartet. EMI CDC 47126, 47130.

Sonata in B-flat, Op. 106 (Hammerklavier). Maurizio Pollini, pianist. DG 429 569-2.

Diabelli Variations, Op. 120. Rudolph Serkin, pianist. Sony MK44 837.